SCOTTISH CERTIFICATE OF EDUCATION

Higher
CHEMISTRY

The Scottish Certificate of Education Examination Papers
are reprinted by special permission of
THE SCOTTISH QUALIFICATIONS AUTHORITY

Note: The answers to the questions do not emanate from the Authority.

ISBN 0 7169 9278 7
© *Robert Gibson & Sons, Glasgow, Ltd., 1998*

ROBERT GIBSON · Publisher
17 Fitzroy Place, Glasgow, G3 7SF.

CONTENTS

SCOTTISH
CERTIFICATE OF
EDUCATION

Time: 1 hour 40 minutes

CHEMISTRY
HIGHER GRADE
Paper I

INSTRUCTIONS TO CANDIDATES

Check that the answer sheet provided is for Chemistry Higher I.

Fill in the details required on the answer sheet.

Reference may be made to the Chemistry (Revised) Higher Grade and Certificate of Sixth Year Studies Data Booklet (1992 edition).

Rough working, if required, should be done only on this question paper, or on the rough working sheet provided—**not** on the answer sheet.

Instructions for the completion of **Part 1** and **Part 2** are given on separate pages.

PART 1

In questions 1 to 40 of this part of the paper, an answer is given by indicating the choice A, B, C or D by a stroke made in INK in the appropriate place in Part 1 of the answer sheet—see the sample question below.

For each question there is only ONE correct answer.

This part of the paper is worth 40 marks.

SAMPLE QUESTION

To show that the ink in a ball-pen consists of a mixture of dyes, the method of separation would be

      A   fractional distillation

      B   chromatography

      C   fractional crystallisation

      D   filtration.

The correct answer is B—chromatography. A **heavy** vertical line should be drawn joining the two dots in the appropriate box in the column headed **B** as shown **in the example on the answer sheet**.

If, after you have recorded your answer, you decide that you have made an error and wish to make a change, you should cancel the original answer and put a vertical stroke in the box you now consider to be correct. Thus, if you want to change an answer **D** to an answer **B**, your answer sheet would look like this:

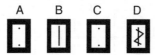

If you want to change back to an answer which has already been scored out, you should **enter a tick (✓)** to the RIGHT of the box of your choice, thus:

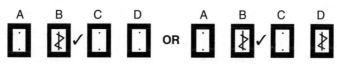

In questions 41 to 48 of this part of the paper, an answer is given by circling the appropriate letter (or letters) in the answer grids provided on Part 2 of the answer sheet.

In some questions, two letters are required for full marks.

If more than the correct number of answers is given, marks will be deducted.

In some cases the number of correct responses is NOT identified in the question.

This part of the paper is worth 20 marks.

SAMPLE QUESTION

A CH_4	B H_2	C CO_2
D CO	E C_2H_6	F N_2

(a) Identify the diatomic **compound(s)**.

A	B	C
(D)	E	F

The one correct answer to part (a) is D. This should be circled.

(b) Identify the **two** substances which burn to produce **both** carbon dioxide **and** water.

(A)	B	C
D	(E)	F

As indicated in this question, there are **two** correct answers to part (b). These are A and E.

Both answers are circled.

(c) Identify the substance(s) which can **not** be used as a fuel.

A	B	(C)
D	E	(F)

There are **two** correct answers to part (c). These are C and F.

Both answers are circled.

If, after you have recorded your answer, you decide that you have made an error and wish to make a change, you should cancel the original answer and circle the answer you now consider to be correct. Thus, in part (a), if you want to change an answer **D** to an answer **A**, your answer sheet would look like this:

(A)	B	C
⌀D̸	E	F

If you want to change back to an answer which has already been scored out, you should enter a tick (✓) in the box of the answer of your choice, thus:

⌀A̸	B	C
✓⌀D̸	E	F

4

SCOTTISH
CERTIFICATE OF
EDUCATION
1995

MONDAY, 15 MAY
9.30 AM – 11.10 AM

CHEMISTRY
HIGHER GRADE
Paper I

INSTRUCTIONS TO CANDIDATES

Check that the answer sheet provided is for Chemistry Higher I.

Fill in the details required on the answer sheet.

Reference may be made to the Chemistry (Revised) Higher Grade and Certificate of Sixth Year Studies Data Booklet (1992 edition).

Rough working, if required, should be done only on this question paper, or on the rough working sheet provided—**not** on the answer sheet.

Instructions for the completion of **Part 1** and **Part 2** are given on separate pages.

PART 1

1. The reaction of copper(II) oxide with dilute sulphuric acid is an example of

   A   oxidation

   B   reduction

   C   neutralisation

   D   displacement.

2. Which pair of solutions is most likely to produce a precipitate when mixed?

   A   Silver nitrate + sodium chloride

   B   Magnesium nitrate + sodium sulphate

   C   Magnesium nitrate + sodium chloride

   D   Silver nitrate + sodium sulphate

3. The reaction

   $$C_6H_{12}O_6 + 6O_2 \rightarrow 6CO_2 + 6H_2O$$

   is an example of

   A   photosynthesis

   B   hydrolysis

   C   combustion

   D   hydration.

4.

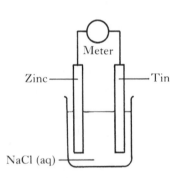

   Which set of observations would apply to this cell?

	Change in mass of zinc	Electron flow through meter
A	lighter	tin to zinc
B	lighter	zinc to tin
C	heavier	tin to zinc
D	heavier	zinc to tin

5. A pupil obtained a certain volume of carbon dioxide by the reaction of 20 cm^3 of 2 mol l^{-1} hydrochloric acid with excess sodium carbonate.

   Which of the following acids would give the same final volume of carbon dioxide when added to excess sodium carbonate?

   A 20 cm^3 of 4 mol l^{-1} hydrochloric acid

   B 10 cm^3 of 4 mol l^{-1} hydrochloric acid

   C 20 cm^3 of 2 mol l^{-1} sulphuric acid

   D 40 cm^3 of 2 mol l^{-1} hydrochloric acid

6. A metal (melting point $843 \,°C$, density $1·54 \text{ g cm}^{-3}$) was obtained by electrolysis of its just molten chloride (melting point $772 \,°C$, density $2·15 \text{ g cm}^{-3}$).

   During the electrolysis, how would the metal occur?

   A   As a solid on the surface of the electrolyte

   B   As a liquid on the surface of the electrolyte

   C   As a solid at the bottom of the electrolyte

   D   As a liquid at the bottom of the electrolyte

7. Part of a polymer is shown.

   $$-\overset{\underset{|}{H}}{\underset{|}{C}}-\overset{\underset{|}{C_2H_5}}{\underset{|}{C}}-\overset{\underset{|}{H}}{\underset{|}{C}}-\overset{\underset{|}{H}}{\underset{|}{C}}-\overset{\underset{|}{H}}{\underset{|}{C}}-\overset{\underset{|}{C_2H_5}}{\underset{|}{C}}-\overset{\underset{|}{H}}{\underset{|}{C}}-\overset{\underset{|}{H}}{\underset{|}{C}}-$$

   Which pair of alkenes was used as monomers?

   A   Ethene and propene

   B   Ethene and but-1-ene

   C   Propene and but-1-ene

   D   Ethene and but-2-ene

8. 1 mol of hydrogen gas and 1 mol of iodine vapour were mixed and allowed to react. After t seconds, $0·8$ mol of hydrogen remained.

   The number of moles of hydrogen iodide formed at t seconds was

   A $0·2$

   B $0·4$

   C $0·8$

   D $1·6$.

9. Graph **X** was obtained when 1 g of calcium carbonate powder reacted with excess dilute hydrochloric acid at 20 °C.

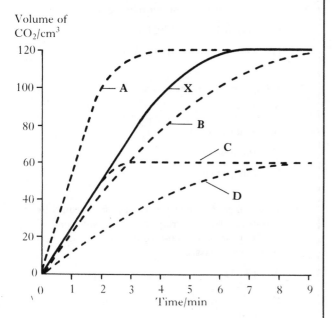

Which curve would best represent the reaction of 0·5 g lump calcium carbonate with excess of the same dilute hydrochloric acid?

10. The potential energy diagram for the reaction

$$CO(g) + NO_2(g) \rightarrow CO_2(g) + NO(g)$$

is shown.

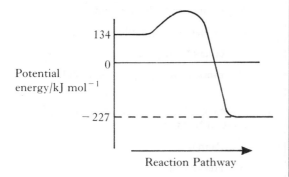

ΔH, in kJ mol^{-1}, for the reaction is

A -361

B -227

C -93

D $+361$.

11. Which of the following describes the effect of a catalyst?

	Activation energy	Enthalpy of reaction
A	decreased	decreased
B	decreased	no change
C	no change	decreased
D	decreased	increased

12. What compound is formed by the oxidation of propan-2-ol?

A CH_3CH_2CHO

B CH_3COCH_3

C CH_3CH_2COOH

D $CH_3CH_2CH_2OH$

13. Ethanol vapour is passed over hot aluminium oxide.

What kind of reaction occurs?

A Hydrogenation

B Dehydration

C Hydrolysis

D Dehydrogenation

14. One of the main methods for the production of diesel is

A blending of naphtha fractions

B reforming of naphtha fractions

C reforming of gas oil fractions

D blending of gas oil fractions.

15.

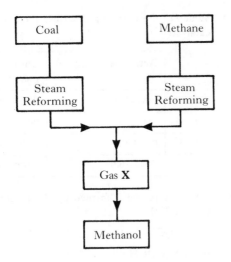

Gas **X**, a feedstock for the manufacture of methanol, is

A   methanal

B   hydrogen

C   carbon monoxide

D   synthesis gas.

16. The equation for the complete combustion of propane is

$$C_3H_8(g) + 5O_2(g) \rightarrow 3CO_2(g) + 4H_2O(\ell).$$

50 cm^3 of propane is mixed with 500 cm^3 of oxygen and the mixture is ignited.

What is the volume of the resulting gas mixture? (All volumes are measured at the same temperature and pressure.)

A   150 cm^3

B   300 cm^3

C   400 cm^3

D   700 cm^3

17. The density of chlorine gas is found to be $3 \cdot 00$ g l^{-1}.

Under the experimental conditions, the molar volume, in litres, is

A $11 \cdot 8$

B $22 \cdot 4$

C $23 \cdot 7$

D $35 \cdot 5$.

18. Avogadro's constant is the same as the number of

A   molecules in 1 mol of oxygen gas

B   atoms in 1 mol of hydrogen gas

C   ions in 1 mol of NaCl

D   electrons in 1 mol of helium gas.

19. 160 g of calcium contains as many atoms as

A   28 g of carbon

B   92 g of sodium

C   160 g of silver

D   256 g of sulphur.

20. What mass of copper metal, in grams, would be deposited by electrolysis of a solution of Cu^{2+}(aq) ions if 1000 coulombs of electrical charge were passed?

A   12 352

B $3 \cdot 3$

C $0 \cdot 66$

D $0 \cdot 33$

21. The compound with formula

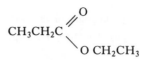

CH$_3$CH$_2$C

can be made from

A   ethanol and ethanoic acid

B   propan-1-ol and ethanoic acid

C   ethanol and propanoic acid

D   propan-1-ol and propanoic acid.

22. Which of the following decolourises bromine solution **least** rapidly?

A   Palm oil

B   Hex-1-ene

C   Cod liver oil

D   Mutton fat

23. When two amino acids condense together, water is eliminated and a peptide link is formed.

Which of the following represents this process?

A

B

C

D

24. Proteins can be denatured under acid conditions.

During this denaturing, the protein molecule

A   changes shape

B   is dehydrated

C   is neutralised

D   is polymerised.

25. Which type of structure is found in a substance melting at 771 K which conducts electricity when molten, but not when solid?

A   Covalent (discrete molecules)

B   Covalent (network structure)

C   Ionic

D   Metallic

26. The spike graph shows the variation in the first ionisation energy with atomic number for sixteen consecutive elements in the Periodic Table. The element at which the spike graph starts is **not** specified.

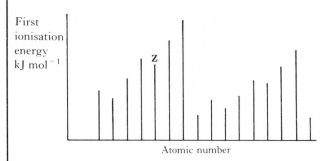

In which group of the Periodic Table is element **Z**?

A   1

B   3

C   5

D   6

27. Which of the following chlorides is likely to have **least** ionic character?

A $BeCl_2$

B $CaCl_2$

C $LiCl$

D $CsCl$

28. Which equation represents the first ionisation energy of a diatomic element, X_2?

A $\frac{1}{2}X_2(s) \rightarrow X^+(g)$

B $\frac{1}{2}X_2(g) \rightarrow X^-(g)$

C $X(s) \rightarrow X^-(g)$

D $X(g) \rightarrow X^+(g)$

29. Molten lithium hydride can be electrolysed using platinum electrodes.

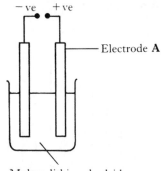

Molten lithium hydride

What is the reaction taking place at electrode **A**?

A $2H^-(\ell) \rightarrow H_2(g) + 2e$

B $2H^+(\ell) + 2e \rightarrow H_2(g)$

C $Li^+(\ell) + e \rightarrow Li(\ell)$

D $Li(\ell) \rightarrow Li^+(\ell) + e$

30. In which of the following would a displacement reaction take place?

A Bubbling chlorine gas through an aqueous solution of sodium fluoride

B Adding bromine solution to an aqueous solution of sodium chloride

C Adding bromine solution to an aqueous solution of sodium fluoride

D Bubbling chlorine gas through an aqueous solution of sodium iodide

31.

Bond	Bond enthalpy/kJ mol^{-1}
H—H	436
I—I	151
H—I	299

$$H_2(g) + I_2(g) \rightarrow 2HI(g)$$

What is the enthalpy of reaction, in kJ mol^{-1}, for the above reaction?

A +11

B −11

C +288

D −288

32. Here are some enthalpy changes relating to chlorine.

ΔH_1 — hydration enthalpy of chloride ions
ΔH_2 — first ionisation energy of chlorine
ΔH_3 — bond enthalpy of Cl — Cl bond
ΔH_4 — electron gain enthalpy (affinity) of chlorine

$$\tfrac{1}{2}Cl_2(g) \rightarrow Cl^-(g)$$

Which of these enthalpy changes are needed to calculate the enthalpy change for the above process?

A ΔH_1 and ΔH_4

B ΔH_2 and ΔH_3

C ΔH_3 and ΔH_4

D ΔH_2 and ΔH_4

33. The mean bond enthalpy of a C—F bond is 486 kJ mol^{-1}.

In which of the processes is ΔH approximately equal to +1944 kJ mol^{-1}?

A $CF_4(g) \rightarrow C(s) + 2F_2(g)$

B $CF_4(g) \rightarrow C(g) + 4F(g)$

C $CF_4(g) \rightarrow C(g) + 2F_2(g)$

D $CF_4(g) \rightarrow C(s) + 4F(g)$

34. Chemical reactions are in a state of dynamic equilibrium only when

A   the rate of the forward reaction equals that of the backward reaction

B   the concentrations of reactants and products are equal

C   the activation energies of the forward and backward reactions are equal

D   the reaction involves no enthalpy change.

35. Under the conditions used industrially, ethene and steam react as follows.

$$C_2H_4(g) + H_2O(g) \rightarrow C_2H_5OH(g)$$
$$\Delta H = -46 \text{ kJ mol}^{-1}$$

Which set of conditions would give the best yield of ethanol at equilibrium?

A   High temperature, low pressure

B   High temperature, high pressure

C   Low temperature, high pressure

D   Low temperature, low pressure

36. Which of the following is the same for equal volumes of equimolar solutions of sodium hydroxide and ammonia?

A   pH of solution

B   Mass of solute present

C   Conductivity of solution

D   Moles of acid needed for complete reaction

37. β-particles emitted by certain radioactive atoms are

A   electrons from the outer shell

B   electrons from the nucleus

C   particles consisting of 2 protons and 2 neutrons

D   electromagnetic radiations of very short wavelength.

38. $^{27}_{13}Al$ can absorb an α-particle with the emission of a neutron.

What is the product of this reaction?

A $^{30}_{14}Si$

B $^{28}_{15}P$

C $^{30}_{15}P$

D $^{31}_{16}S$

39. Plants take in radon with water through their roots.

Compared with radon in the water, the half-life of the radon in the plant cells will be

A   shorter

B   longer

C   the same

D   dependent on the size of the plant.

40. The half-life of the isotope ^{14}C is 5.5×10^3 years.

What fraction of the original ^{14}C atoms will be present after 2.2×10^4 years?

A   0.5

B   0.25

C   0.125

D   0.0625

PART 2

41. The grid shows concentrations of solutions in mol l^{-1}.

A	B	C
1×10^{-1}	1×10^{-3}	1×10^{-6}
D	E	F
1×10^{-8}	1×10^{-11}	1×10^{-13}

(a) Identify the concentration of hydroxide ions in a solution of sodium hydroxide with a pH of 11.

(b) Identify the concentration of hydrogen ions in a solution made by pipetting $1 \cdot 0 \, \text{cm}^3$ of $0 \cdot 001$ mol l^{-1} hydrochloric acid into a litre standard flask and making up with distilled water.

42.

A	B	C
H—C—C—C—C—H (with O double bond and H's)	H—C—C—C—C—OH (with H's)	H—C—C—C—C—H (with OH on third C)
D	**E**	**F**
cyclic structure H—C—C with =O, H—C—C—H	H—C—C—C—C—H (with OH on third C)	H—C—C—C—C=O (with H's)

(a) Identify the compound which can be oxidised to produce the compound shown in box **F**.

(b) Identify the isomer of the compound shown in box **C**.

(c) Identify the **two** ketones.

43.

A	B	C
$NH_4Cl(s)$	$CH_3OH(\ell)$	$C_6H_{14}(\ell)$
D	E	F
$KOH(s)$	$Na_2CO_3(s)$	$SiO_2(s)$

(a) Identify the covalent network substance.

(b) Identify the substance which contains hydrogen bonds.

(c) Identify the substance(s) which when added to water would produce an alkaline solution.

44. Oil of wintergreen and aspirin are used in medicine. Their structures are shown below.

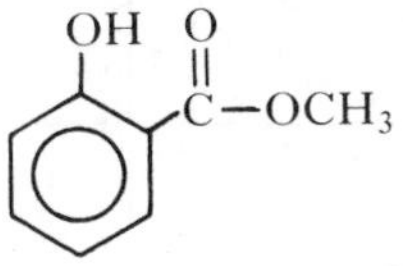

Oil of wintergreen 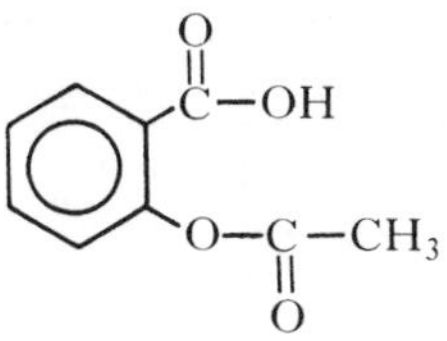   Aspirin

A		B		C	
	hydrocarbon		aromatic		aldehyde
D		E		F	
	alcohol		carboxylic acid		ester

(a) Identify the term which can be applied to aspirin but **not** to oil of wintergreen.

(b) Identify the term(s) which can be applied to **both** aspirin and oil of wintergreen.

45. Proteins and fats are hydrolysed during digestion.

A		B		C	
	$C_{17}H_{35}-C\lessgtr^{O}_{OH}$		$CH_3-\overset{O}{\overset{\|}{C}}-OC_2H_5$		$\underset{OH\quad OH\quad OH}{CH_2-CH-CH_2}$
D		E		F	
	$C_2H_5-C\lessgtr^{O}_{OH}$		$C_3H_7-NH_2$		$H_2N-CH_2-C\lessgtr^{O}_{OH}$

(a) Identify the compound which could be produced by the hydrolysis of a protein.

(b) Identify the compound(s) which could be produced by the hydrolysis of a fat.

46.

A	B	C
carbon monoxide	ethanol	hydrogen

D	E	F
ammonia	methane	water

(*a*) Identify the **two** substances which would be gaseous at room temperature and made up of molecules which are **not** diatomic.

(*b*) Identify the substance(s) which would be made up of non-polar molecules.

47. Carbon dioxide is produced in respiration.

Identify the **true** statement(s) about carbon dioxide.

A	The mass of 6.02×10^{23} molecules of the gas is 44 g.
B	44 g of the gas contains 6.02×10^{23} atoms.
C	One molecule of the gas is 44 times as heavy as a molecule of hydrogen.
D	44 g of the gas occupies the same volume as 16 g of oxygen, under the same conditions.
E	44 g of the gas contains the same number of atoms as 60 g of neon.
F	One molecule of the gas has a mass of 44 g.

[END OF QUESTION PAPER]

SCOTTISH
CERTIFICATE OF
EDUCATION
1995

MONDAY, 15 MAY
1.30 PM – 4.30 PM

CHEMISTRY
HIGHER GRADE
Paper II

Marks

1. The radioisotope, sodium-24, can be made in a nuclear reactor by bombarding element **X** with neutrons.

$$^a_b X \; + \; ^1_0 n \; \longrightarrow \; ^{24}_{11} Na$$

(*a*) Identify element **X** and write values for **a** and **b**.

X is Na
a = 23
b = 11

1

(*b*) The graph shows how the mass of a sample of sodium-24 varies with time.

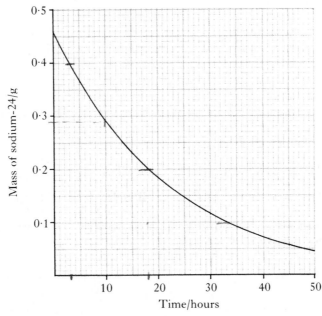

(i) What is the half-life of sodium-24?

18 - 3 = 15 hours

1

(ii) Calculate the average rate of decay of sodium-24 over the first ten hours.
(Show your working clearly.)

0·46 − 0·29 = 0·17   10 × 60 = 600 × 60 = 36,000

$$\frac{0·17}{36000} =$$

1

15

Marks

(iii) If the temperature of the sodium-24 sample is increased, how would this affect its rate of decay?

It has no affect on the rate of decay

1

(c) Two samples of ^{24}Na and $^{24}NaCl$ have the same mass.

Why are their intensities of radiation different?

1
(5)

2. Rechargeable nickel-cadmium cells are widely used in portable electronic equipment.

When such a cell is **discharging**, the following half-reactions take place.

$$Cd(s) + 2OH^-(aq) \longrightarrow Cd(OH)_2(s) + 2e$$

$$Ni(OH)_3(s) + e \longrightarrow Ni(OH)_2(s) + OH^-(aq) \qquad \times 2$$

(a) Combine the half-reactions to write a balanced equation for the reaction which takes place when this cell is discharging.

$$Cd(s) + 2Ni(OH)_3(s) + 2OH^-(aq) \rightarrow Cd(OH)_2(s) +$$

$$Cd(s) + 2Ni(OH)_3(s) \rightarrow Cd(OH)_2(s) \qquad 2Ni(OH)_2(s)$$
$$+ 2Ni(OH)_2(s) \qquad + 2OH^-(aq)$$

1

(b) What effect would **recharging** the cell have on the above half-reactions?

Reverse them

1
(2)

Marks

3. The germanes are a homologous series of germanium hydrides, similar to the alkanes.

The simplest is monogermane, GeH_4. It can be prepared by the reaction of germanium(IV) chloride with lithium aluminium hydride, $LiAlH_4$. Both lithium chloride and aluminium chloride are also produced in the reaction.

(*a*) What is meant by a homologous series?

> A series with the same general formula and characteristics for each member.

1

(*b*) What would be the shape of a monogermane molecule?

> A tetrahedral

1

(*c*) Write a balanced equation for the production of monogermane as outlined in the above reaction.

> $4GeCl_4 + 4LiAlH_4 \rightarrow 4GeH_4 + 4LiCl + AlCl_3$

1

(*d*) Draw the full structural formula for trigermane.

1
(4)

Marks

4. Three experiments were carried out in a study of the rate of reaction between magnesium (in excess) and dilute hydrochloric acid. A balance was used to record the mass of the reaction flask and its contents. The results of Experiment 1, using 0.4 mol l^{-1} acid, are shown in the graph.

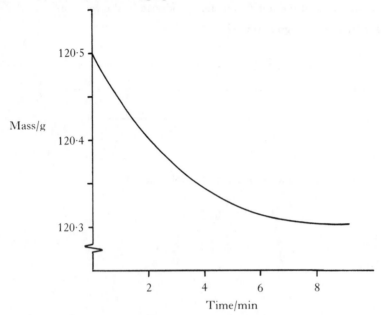

(*a*) Why did the balance record a decrease in mass during the reaction?

1

(*b*) The **only** difference between Experiment 2 and Experiment 1 was the use of a catalyst.
On the above graph, sketch a curve that could be expected for Experiment 2 (label 2).

1

(*c*) The **only** difference between Experiment 3 and Experiment 1 was the use of 0.2 mol l^{-1} acid.
On the above graph, sketch a curve that could be expected for Experiment 3 (label 3).

1

(3)

Marks

5. The flow diagram shows how vinyl chloride (CH_2=CHCl), an important feedstock, is made in industry.

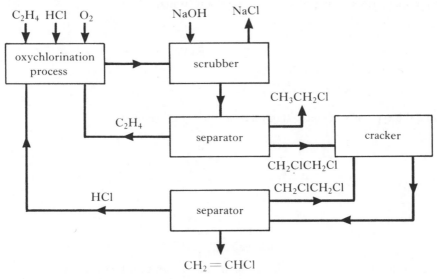

(a) (i) What is the systematic name for vinyl chloride?

1

(ii) Give a use for vinyl chloride.

plastics

1

(b) Write the formulae for the **three** substances which are recycled.

C_2H_4 , HCl , CH_2ClCH_2Cl

1

(c) Write the equation for the reaction taking place in the cracker.

1

Marks

(*d*) Name the process taking place in the separator units.

distillation

1

(*e*) Name the type of reaction taking place in the scrubber unit.

1
(6)

6.   *Markovnikoff's Rule*

Addition of hydrogen chloride to an alkene can give two products.

Markovnikoff observed that the hydrogen of the hydrogen chloride mainly attaches to the carbon atom of the double bond which already has the most hydrogens **directly** attached to it.

(*a*) Draw the full structural formula for the major product formed when hydrogen chloride reacts with propene.

HCl +

1

(*b*) Why is it not necessary to consider Markovnikoff's rule when hydrogen chloride reacts with but-2-ene?

1
(2)

Marks

7. Diamond and graphite are forms of carbon with very different properties.

Graphite can mark paper, is a lubricant and is a conductor of electricity.

Diamond has none of these properties.

(*a*) Draw a diagram to show the structure of diamond.

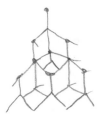

1

(*b*) Why is graphite an effective lubricant?

It is slippery because the layers slide over each other

1

(*c*) A pupil uses a graphite pencil to write her signature 100 times on a piece of weighed paper.

Results			
	Number of signatures	=	100
	Mass of blank paper	=	4·895 g
	Mass of paper + 100 signatures	=	4·905 g

Use her results to calculate the number of carbon atoms present in one signature.

(Show your working clearly.)

2

Marks

(*d*) Boron nitride can form a similar strucure to graphite. The boron and nitrogen atoms alternate throughout the structure as shown.

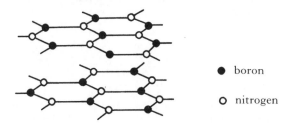

● boron

○ nitrogen

(i) Why is this substance a non-conductor, while graphite is a conductor?

1

(ii) Suggest why the bonds between the layers in boron nitride are stronger than the bonds between the layers in graphite.

1

(6)

8. Members of a homologous series contain the same functional group.

(*a*) What is meant by a functional group?

1

(*b*) A student carried out four tests on ethanol and ethanoic acid to compare the properties of the two homologous series, alcohols and carboxylic acids.

The tests are illustrated below.

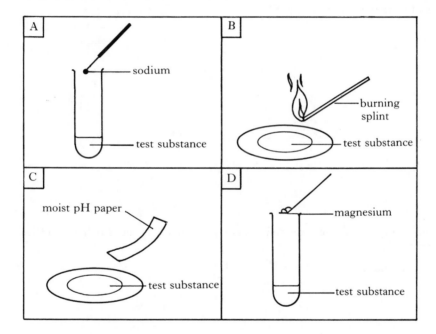

(i) Choose **one** test in which ethanol and ethanoic acid give different results and state the results.

1

(ii) Choose **another** test in which ethanol and ethanoic acid give a similar result and state the result.

1

(*c*) Ethanol can be oxidised to compound **X** which can be further oxidised to ethanoic acid.

Name compound **X**.

1

(*d*) Ethanol can be classified as a primary alcohol.

Name an alcohol which can be classified as a secondary alcohol.

1
(5)

Marks

9. A page of a pupil's notebook shows instructions on how to measure the enthalpy of combustion of an alcohol.

> ### *Experimental procedure*
>
> *1. Measure out 100 cm³ of water into a beaker.*
>
> *2. Take steps to insulate the apparatus.*
>
> *3. Read the water temperature before and after using the alcohol burner to heat it.*
>
> *4. Weigh the alcohol burner before and after the experiment.*

(a) Draw a neat labelled diagram of the apparatus which the pupil could use to carry out this experiment.

2

(b) Write the equation corresponding to the enthalpy of combustion of methanol.

1

(c) The pupil found that when 0·23 g of methanol burned, the heat produced raised the temperature of 100 g of water by 9·2 °C.

Using information on page 7 of the data booklet, calculate the enthalpy of combustion of methanol.

(Show your working clearly.)

2

(d) The pupil's result is well below the value in the data booklet. Even with insulation, much heat is lost to the surroundings, including the apparatus. Suggest one **other** reason why the experimental result is low.

1

(6)

Marks

10. The following apparatus can be used to determine the relative formula masses of liquids which are easily evaporated.

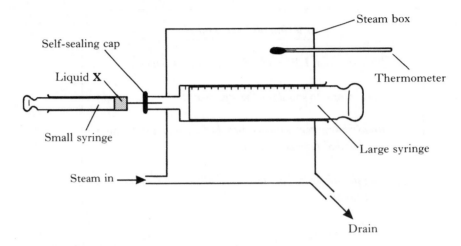

Some of liquid **X** is injected into the large syringe and it evaporates.
The following results were obtained:

Mass of small syringe before injection   =   5·774 g
Mass of small syringe after injection   =   5·648 g
Large syringe reading before injection =   5 cm³
Large syringe reading after injection   =   89 cm³

(*a*) Calculate the relative formula mass of liquid **X**.

(Take the molar volume of a gas to be 30·6 litre mol⁻¹.)

(Show your working clearly.)

2

(*b*) Suggest why the above apparatus could **not** be used to determine the relative formula masses of liquids with boiling points above 100 °C.

1

(3)

Marks

11. A ratio line can be used to illustrate the carbon to hydrogen ratio in different compounds.

carbon to hydrogen ratio

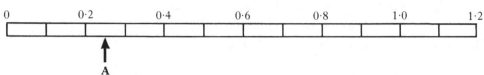

Methane would appear at point **A**.

(*a*) At what value on the line would butane appear?

1

(*b*) A hydrocarbon **X** with six carbon atoms per molecule has a carbon to hydrogen ratio of 0·5. **X** does **not** immediately decolourise bromine solution.

Give a name for **X**.

1

(*c*) Reforming is an industrial process which can convert alkanes into aromatic hydrocarbons.

(i) In relation to the alkane hydrocarbons, where on the line would the reformed hydrocarbons appear?

1

(ii) Name the aromatic hydrocarbon produced by reforming hexane.

1

(iii) Explain why the demand for fuel with a higher aromatic content has increased in the last ten years.

2

(6)

Marks

12. The first noble gas compound, xenon hexafluoroplatinate(V), was prepared in 1962 by Professor Neil Bartlett, a British scientist working in Canada.

$$Xe(g) + PtF_6(g) \longrightarrow Xe^+PtF_6^-(s) \qquad \Delta H = 0 \text{ kJ mol}^{-1}$$
xenon hexafluoroplatinate(V)

(*a*) The energy diagram for this reaction is illustrated below.

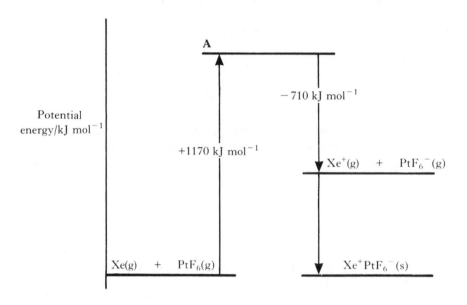

(i) On the line marked **A**, write the appropriate symbols and formulae.

$$Xe(g) \rightarrow Xe(g)^+ + e^-$$

1

(ii) Calculate the lattice-making enthalpy of $Xe^+PtF_6^-(s)$.

$$1170 = 710 + ?$$
$$1170 - 710 =$$

1

(*b*) Xenon(VI) fluoride is another noble gas compound. It can be prepared directly from its elements.

$$Xe(g) + 3F_2(g) \longrightarrow XeF_6(g) \qquad \Delta H = -329 \text{ kJ mol}^{-1}$$

(i) What name is given to this kind of enthalpy change?

exothermic

1

(ii) Using information on bond enthalpies from the data booklet, calculate the bond enthalpy of the $Xe - F$ bond in XeF_6.

(Show your working clearly.)

$$6 \times Xe - F$$
$$6 \times$$

2

(5)

28

Marks

13. (*a*) Esters are formed when carboxylic acids react with alcohols, e.g.

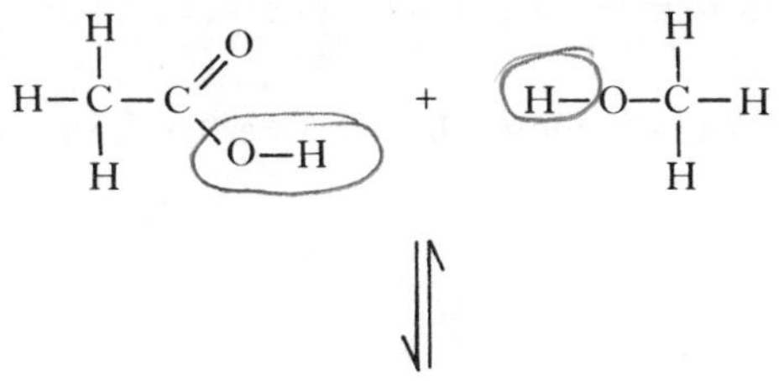

$$\Big\Updownarrow$$

ester   + H_2O

(i) Name the ester formed in this reaction.

methyl ethanoate

1

(ii) Name the type of reaction which takes place.

condensation

1

(iii) To find out which atoms of the alcohol and carboxylic acid go to form the water molecule, the reaction was carried out using an alcohol in which the ^{16}O atom was substituted by the ^{18}O isotope. All of the ^{18}O was found in the ester and none in the water.

In the equation above, circle the atoms in the acid and the alcohol which combine to form the water molecule.

1

Marks

(b) Esters can be prepared in the laboratory by heating an alcohol and a carboxylic acid with a few drops of concentrated sulphuric acid in a water bath. After 10 minutes or so, the reaction mixture is poured into sodium hydrogencarbonate solution.

(i) What evidence, apart from smell, shows that the ester has been formed?

A seperate layer

1

(ii) State **two** safety precautions that should be adopted when carrying out this experiment.

1

(c) Bucrylate is an ester which is used in surgery for repairing torn tissue.

$$H-\overset{\displaystyle H}{\underset{}{C}}=\overset{\displaystyle CN}{\underset{\displaystyle \underset{O}{\parallel}}{C}}-C-O-CH_2-\overset{}{\underset{\displaystyle CH_3}{CH}}-CH_3$$

It instantaneously polymerises when it comes in contact with ionic solutions.

(i) What type of polymerisation will bucrylate undergo?

1

(ii) Draw the structure of the **repeating unit** in polybucrylate.

1
(7)

Marks

14. In the Birkeland-Eyde Process, nitrogen and oxygen combine on sparking to produce nitrogen monoxide.

$$\tfrac{1}{2}N_2(g) + \tfrac{1}{2}O_2(g) \rightleftharpoons NO(g) \qquad \Delta H_f = +100 \text{ kJ mol}^{-1}$$

The activation energy for this reaction is 1200 kJ mol^{-1}.

(*a*) Complete the energy-diagram for the industrial process.

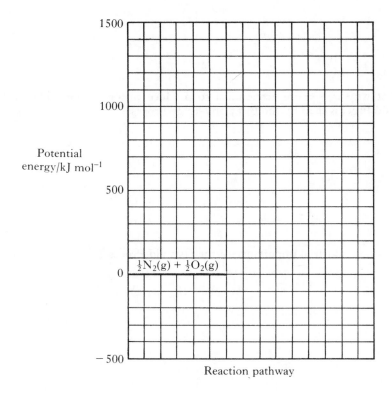

Reaction pathway

2

(*b*) (i) Suggest a feedstock for the Birkeland-Eyde Process.

1

(ii) Explain how an increase in temperature would affect the yield of nitrogen monoxide.

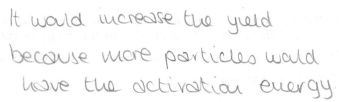

It would increase the yield because more particles would have the activation energy

2

31

(c) In industry, nitrogen monoxide is now produced in the UK by the Ostwald Process.

(i) Name the **two** reactants in the Ostwald Process.

nitrogen , oxygen

1

(ii) Suggest why it is more economical to produce nitrogen monoxide by the Ostwald Process than by the Birkeland-Eyde Process.

1

(iii) What is the industrial importance of the Ostwald Process?

1
(8)

15. The water in swimming pools can be kept sterile by the addition of chlorine which kills microorganisms. The chlorine levels in swimming pool water can be determined by titrating samples against acidified iron(II) sulphate solution. The reaction taking place is:

$$Cl_2(aq) + 2Fe^{2+}(aq) \longrightarrow 2Cl^-(aq) + 2Fe^{3+}(aq)$$

(a) Write the ion-electron equation for the oxidation half-reaction.

$$2Fe^{2+} \longrightarrow 2Fe^{3+} + 2e^-$$

1

(b) A 100 cm³ sample of water from a swimming pool required 24·9 cm³ of $2·82 \times 10^{-4}$ mol l⁻¹ iron(II) sulphate solution to reach the end-point.

Calculate the chlorine concentration, in g l⁻¹, in the swimming pool water.

(Show your working clearly.)

3
(4)

Marks

16. Three dichlorobenzene isomers are known. Their structures depend on the positions of the chlorine atoms in the benzene ring. Two of the isomers are shown.

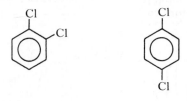

A   1,2 dichlorobenzene   **B**   1,4 dichlorobenzene

(*a*) Draw the structure of the third isomer and name it.

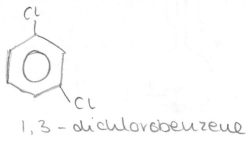

1, 3 - dichlorobenzene

1

(*b*) Give the molecular formula for the three isomers.

1

(*c*) Why is molecule **A** polar while molecule **B** is not polar?

Because B is symmetrical and A isn't.

1
(3)

Marks

17. Tin iodide can be prepared directly from its elements.

Excess tin is heated for about an hour with iodine dissolved in tetrachloromethane.

Tetrachloromethane, which has a boiling point of 77 °C, acts as a solvent both for the iodine and for the tin iodide that is formed.

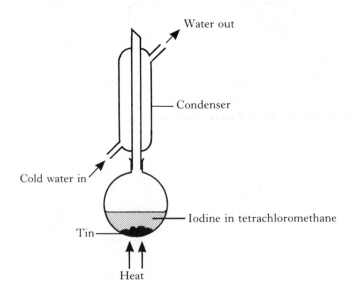

When the reaction is complete, the excess tin is removed. On cooling the remaining solution, orange crystals of tin iodide appear.

The crystals have a melting point of 144 °C.

(*a*) Why is a condenser used when heating the reaction mixture?

To stop gases being removed.

1

(*b*) (i) Give **two** pieces of evidence from the method of preparation which suggest that tin iodide is a discrete molecular covalent compound.

2

(ii) What type of bonds would be broken when tin iodide melts?

1

(c) The following results were obtained in the experiment.

$$
\begin{aligned}
\text{Mass of iodine} \quad &= 6\cdot34 \text{ g} \\
\text{Initial mass of tin} \quad &= 3\cdot60 \text{ g} \\
\text{Final mass of tin} \quad &= 2\cdot13 \text{ g}
\end{aligned}
$$

Use the data to calculate the empirical formula for tin iodide.

(Show your working clearly.)

2

(d) Tin iodide reacts readily with water to produce an acidic gas.

Name the gas that is formed in this reaction.

1

(7)

Marks

18. Trichloromethane is insoluble in water. When ammonia is added to a beaker containing water and trichloromethane, the ammonia dissolves in both solvents giving different concentrations.

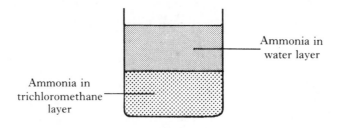

The ratio

$$\frac{\text{concentration of ammonia in water}}{\text{concentration of ammonia in trichloromethane}}$$

is called the partition coefficient.

This can be found by titrating the ammonia in each layer against dilute hydrochloric acid.

(*a*) Write an equation to show why an aqueous solution of ammonia is a weak alkali.

1

(*b*) (i) How could the end-points of the titrations be observed?

1

(ii) The concentration of ammonia in water was calculated from three titrations. The titre volumes were as follows.

1st	24·7 cm³
2nd	24·0 cm³
3rd	23·9 cm³

What volume of dilute hydrochloric acid would be used to calculate the concentration of ammonia in water?

1

(iii) The concentration of ammonia in water was found to be 1·7 mol l⁻¹. For the ammonia in trichloromethane, it was found that 18·4 cm³ of dilute hydrochloric acid, concentration 0·050 mol l⁻¹ was required to neutralise 20·0 cm³ of the ammonia solution.

Calculate the value for the partition coefficient of ammonia between water and trichloromethane.

(Show your working clearly.)

2

(5)

19. X-ray diffraction is a technique used to determine the structures of molecules. It is the electrons in the atoms of the molecule which diffract the X-rays. From the diffraction pattern, an electron-density contour map of the molecule can be constructed.

The following map was obtained using an aromatic compound with molecular formula $C_6H_3Cl_3O$.

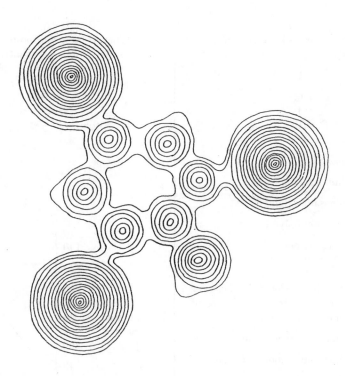

(*a*) Suggest why the hydrogen atoms do not show up clearly in the electron-density contour map.

1

(*b*) Draw the full structural formula for this compound.

1

(*c*) Draw the electron-density contour map that would be obtained for methanoic acid:

$$H-C\overset{\displaystyle O}{\underset{\displaystyle O-H}{\diagup}}$$

1

(3)

[END OF QUESTION PAPER]

PART 1

1. A part of the formula for PTFE is shown.

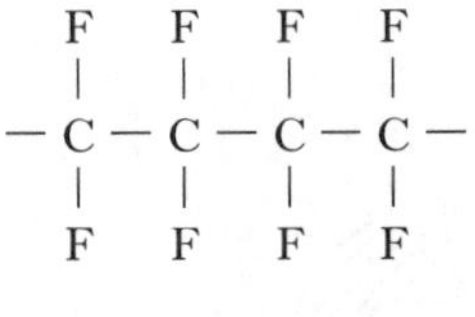

$$-\overset{\overset{\displaystyle F}{|}}{\underset{\underset{\displaystyle F}{|}}{C}}-\overset{\overset{\displaystyle F}{|}}{\underset{\underset{\displaystyle F}{|}}{C}}-\overset{\overset{\displaystyle F}{|}}{\underset{\underset{\displaystyle F}{|}}{C}}-\overset{\overset{\displaystyle F}{|}}{\underset{\underset{\displaystyle F}{|}}{C}}-$$

This polymer is classed as a

A   synthetic addition polymer

B   synthetic condensation polymer

C   natural condensation polymer

D   natural addition polymer.

2. Which of the procedures would be best for obtaining sodium chloride from a mixture of sodium chloride and silver chloride?

A   Add water, filter and collect residue.

B   Add water, filter, and evaporate filtrate.

C   Add hydrochloric acid, filter and collect residue.

D   Add sodium hydroxide solution, filter and evaporate residue.

3. Which gas would react with an acid solution?

A SO_2

B NH_3

C CO_2

D CH_4

4. On analysis, a compound was found to have the following percentage composition by mass.

   Tin 78·8 %   Oxygen 21·2 %

This compound has the formula

A Sn_2O

B SnO

C SnO_2

D Sn_2O_3.

5. What volume of sodium hydroxide solution, concentration $0·4\,mol\,l^{-1}$, is needed to neutralise $50\,cm^3$ of sulphuric acid, concentration $0·1\,mol\,l^{-1}$?

A $25\,cm^3$

B $50\,cm^3$

C $100\,cm^3$

D $200\,cm^3$

6.

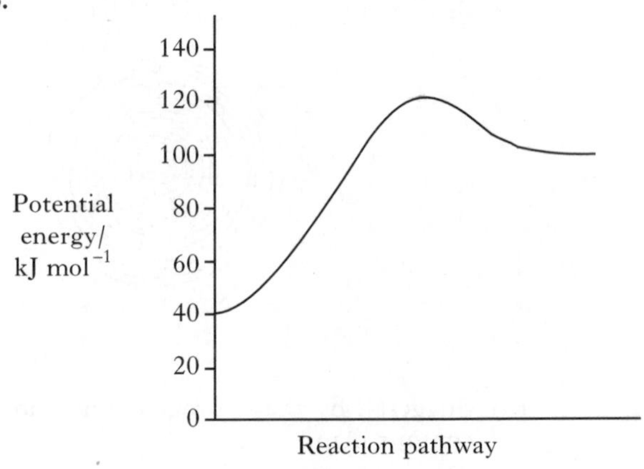

Which set of data applies to the above reaction?

	Enthalpy change	Activation energy/ $kJ\,mol^{-1}$
A	Exothermic	60
B	Exothermic	80
C	Endothermic	60
D	Endothermic	80

7.

Number of
molecules

Kinetic energy E_A

In area X

A molecules always form an activated complex

B no molecules have the energy to form an activated complex

C collisions between molecules are always successful in forming products

D all molecules have the energy to form an activated complex.

8. Liquefied petroleum gas (LPG) is generally a mixture of

A methane and ethane

B ethane and propane

C propane and butane

D butane and octane.

9. Which of the following is an aldehyde?

A

B

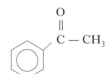

C

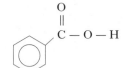

D

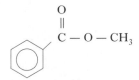

10. Which of the alcohols can be oxidised to give a ketone?

A 2-methylbutan-1-ol

B 2, 3-dimethylpentan-1-ol

C 3-methylbutan-2-ol

D 2-methylbutan-2-ol

11. The conversion of linoleic acid, $C_{18}H_{32}O_2$, into stearic acid, $C_{18}H_{36}O_2$, is likely to be achieved by

A hydrogenation

B hydrolysis

C hydration

D dehydrogenation.

12. The number of moles of ions in 1 mol of copper(II) phosphate is

A 1

B 2

C 4

D 5.

13. Which of the following has the same volume as 14 g of nitrogen gas?

(All volumes are measured under the same conditions of temperature and pressure.)

A 14 g of ethane gas

B 20 g of neon gas

C 22 g of carbon dioxide gas

D 28 g of carbon monoxide gas

14. Potassium nitrate decomposes on heating to give potassium nitrite and oxygen.

$$KNO_3(s) \rightarrow KNO_2(s) + \tfrac{1}{2}O_2(g)$$

What volume of oxygen would be obtained by the decomposition of 0·05 mol of potassium nitrate in such a reaction?

(The molar volume of oxygen under these conditions is 24 litres mol^{-1}.)

A 0·3 litres

B 0·6 litres

C 0·9 litres

D 1·2 litres

15. The mass of 1 mol of sodium is 23 g.
What is the mass of one sodium atom?

A 6×10^{23} g

B 6×10^{-23} g

C 3.8×10^{-23} g

D 3.8×10^{-24} g

16. The Avogadro Constant is the same as the number of

A molecules in 16 g of oxygen

B ions in 1 litre of sodium chloride solution, concentration 1 mol l^{-1}

C atoms in 24 g of carbon

D molecules in 2 g of hydrogen.

17. Rum flavouring is based on the compound with the formula shown.

$$CH_3CH_2CH_2C \overset{O}{\underset{O\,CH_2CH_3}{\big\langle}}$$

It can be made from

A ethanol and butanoic acid

B propanol and ethanoic acid

C butanol and methanoic acid

D propanol and propanoic acid.

18. The production of fatty acids and glycerol from fats in foods is an example of

A hydrolysis

B hydrogenation

C dehydration

D dehydrogenation.

19. Aspirin is one of the most widely used pain relievers in the world. It has the structure:

Which two functional groups are present in an aspirin molecule?

A Hydroxyl and carboxyl

B Aldehyde and ketone

C Carboxyl and ester

D Ester and aldehyde

20. What is the structural formula for glycerol?

A CH_2OH
    $|$
    CH_2
    $|$
    CH_2OH

B CH_2OH
    $|$
    CH_2OH

C CH_2OH
    $|$
    $CHOH$
    $|$
    CH_2COOH

D CH_2OH
    $|$
    $CHOH$
    $|$
    CH_2OH

21.

$$H - \overset{\displaystyle \overset{CH_3}{|}}{\underset{\displaystyle \underset{CH_3}{|}}{C}} - \overset{\displaystyle \overset{NH_2}{|}}{\underset{\displaystyle \underset{H}{|}}{C}} - \overset{\displaystyle O}{C} \overset{\displaystyle \diagup}{\diagdown} {OH}$$

The above molecule can be classified as

A an amino acid

B an ester

C a peptide

D a protein.

22. The rate of hydrolysis of a protein, using an enzyme, was studied at different temperatures. Which graph would be obtained?

A

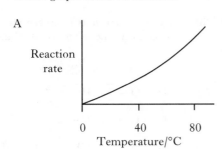

B

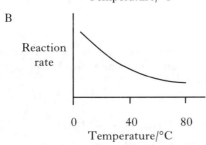

C

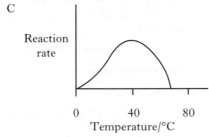

D

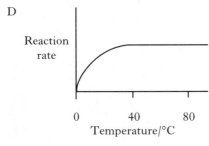

23. The melting points of the Group 7 elements increase on descending the group because the

A covalent bond lengths increase

B mean bond energies increase

C van der Waals attractions increase

D nuclear charges increase.

24. The difference between the covalent radius of sodium and silicon is mainly due to the difference in the

A number of electrons

B number of protons

C number of neutrons

D mass of each atom.

25. Which of the elements is most likely to have a covalent network structure?

Element	Melting point/K	Boiling point/K	Density/ $g\,cm^{-3}$	Conduction when solid?
A	317	553	1·82	No
B	933	2740	2·70	Yes
C	1683	2628	2·32	No
D	387	457	4·93	No

26. In which of the substances, in the solid state, would van der Waals attractions be a significant "intermolecular force"?

A Sodium chloride

B Carbon dioxide

C Magnesium

D Ice

27. Tetrachloromethane, CCl_4, is considered to be a non-polar substance because

A the polar bonds are arranged symmetrically

B the C—Cl bonds are non-polar

C a covalent network structure exists

D only linear molecules are polar.

28. Silicon carbide can be used as

A   a lubricant

B   a tip for cutting/grinding tools

C   a substitute for pencil "lead"

D   an electrical conductor.

29. Which of the processes represents the second ionisation energy of magnesium?

A $Mg^+(g) \rightarrow Mg^{2+}(g) + e$

B $Mg(g) \rightarrow Mg^{2+}(g) + 2e$

C $Mg(s) \rightarrow Mg^{2+}(g) + 2e$

D $Mg^+(s) \rightarrow Mg^{2+}(s) + e$

30. Which of the following represents an exothermic change?

A $O_2(g) \rightarrow 2O(g)$

B $CH_4(g) \rightarrow C(g) + 4H(g)$

C $2N(g) \rightarrow N_2(g)$

D $H_2O(g) \rightarrow 2H(g) + O(g)$

31. The mean bond enthalpy of the C—H bond is $414\,kJ\,mol^{-1}$.

From this information, it can be calculated that 1656 kJ of energy is

A   evolved when 1 mol of methane is burned in excess oxygen

B   required to dissociate 1 mol of methane into free carbon and hydrogen atoms

C   required for the complete combustion of 1 mol of methane

D   evolved when 1 mol of graphite combines with 2 mol of hydrogen gas.

32. $H_2O_2(\ell) \rightarrow H_2O(\ell) + \frac{1}{2}O_2(g)$
$$\Delta H = -52 \text{ kJ mol}^{-1}$$
$H_2(g) + \frac{1}{2}O_2(g) \rightarrow H_2O(\ell)$
$$\Delta H = -286 \text{ kJ mol}^{-1}$$

What is the enthalpy of formation of hydrogen peroxide (H_2O_2)?

A -234 kJ mol^{-1}

B $+234$ kJ mol^{-1}

C -338 kJ mol^{-1}

D $+338$ kJ mol^{-1}

33. Which equation represents the enthalpy of formation of magnesium chloride?

A $Mg(g) + \frac{1}{2}Cl_2(g) \rightarrow MgCl(s)$

B $Mg(s) + Cl_2(g) \rightarrow MgCl_2(s)$

C $Mg(g) + 2Cl(g) \rightarrow MgCl_2(s)$

D $Mg(s) + \frac{1}{2}Cl_2(g) \rightarrow MgCl(g)$

34. Ethanol (C_2H_5OH) has a different enthalpy of combustion from dimethyl ether (CH_3OCH_3). This is because the compounds have different

A   molecular masses

B   bonds within the molecules

C   products of combustion

D   boiling points.

35. On the structure shown, four hydrogen atoms have been replaced by the letters A, B, C and D.

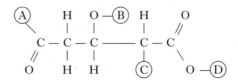

Which letter corresponds to the hydrogen atom which can ionise most easily in aqueous solution?

36. $N_2(g) + 3H_2(g) \rightleftharpoons 2NH_3(g)$

In the Haber Process, illustrated by the equation, the reaction never reaches equilibrium because

A   the ammonia is constantly removed

B   an iron catalyst is used

C   high pressure is used

D   the temperature is held at about 500 °C.

37. The equation refers to the preparation of methanol from synthesis gas.

$$CO(g) + 2H_2(g) \rightleftharpoons CH_3OH(g)$$
$$\Delta H = -91 \text{ kJ mol}^{-1}$$

The formation of methanol is favoured by

A   high pressure and low temperature

B   high pressure and high temperature

C   low pressure and low temperature

D   low pressure and high temperature.

38. Which of the following dissolves in water to give an alkaline solution?

A   Sodium nitrate

B   Potassium ethanoate

C   Ammonium chloride

D   Lithium sulphate

39. A radioactive atom of a Group 5 element emits one β-particle. The decay product will be an atom of an element in

A   Group 3

B   Group 4

C   Group 5

D   Group 6.

40. Which particle will be formed when an atom of $^{211}_{83}$Bi loses an α-particle and the decay product then loses a β-particle?

A $^{210}_{79}$Au

B $^{209}_{80}$Hg

C $^{208}_{81}$Tl

D $^{207}_{82}$Pb

PART 2

41.

A		B		C	
	Condensation		Dehydration		Hydration
D		E		F	
	Hydrolysis		Neutralisation		Precipitation

Identify the kind of reaction which is represented by each of the equations.

(a) $CuO(s) + H_2SO_4(aq) \rightarrow CuSO_4(aq) + H_2O(\ell)$

(b) $NaCl(aq) + AgNO_2(aq) \rightarrow AgCl(s) + NaNO_2(aq)$

(c) $C_2H_4(g) + H_2O(g) \rightarrow C_2H_5OH(\ell)$

42. A pupil carried out three experiments involving the reaction of excess metal with dilute acid. The results of the three experiments are plotted on the graph.

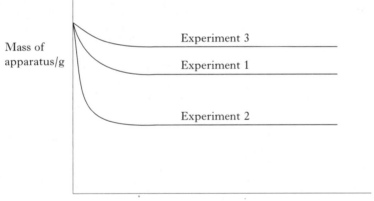

Excess zinc was added to $100\,cm^3$ of $0 \cdot 1\ mol\,l^{-1}$ sulphuric acid in experiment 1.

A		B		C	
	iron/$100\,cm^3$ of $0 \cdot 1\ mol\,l^{-1}$ sulphuric acid		iron/$200\,cm^3$ of $0 \cdot 1\ mol\,l^{-1}$ sulphuric acid		iron/$100\,cm^3$ of $0 \cdot 1\ mol\,l^{-1}$ hydrochloric acid
D		E		F	
	magnesium/$100\,cm^3$ of $0 \cdot 1\ mol\,l^{-1}$ sulphuric acid		magnesium/$200\,cm^3$ of $0 \cdot 2\ mol\,l^{-1}$ hydrochloric acid		magnesium/$100\,cm^3$ of $0 \cdot 2\ mol\,l^{-1}$ hydrochloric acid

(a) Identify the reactants in Experiment 2.

(b) Identify the reactants in Experiment 3.

43.

A	B	C
NH_4^+	Mg^{2+}	OH^-
D	E	F
I^-	Br^-	F^-

Identify the **two** ions which

(a)   react to form an alkaline gas,

(b)   can be displaced from solution by chlorine gas,

(c)   do **not** contain 6.02×10^{24} electrons in one mole of ions.

44.   The first twenty elements in the Periodic Table can be categorised according to their bonding and structure.

A	B	C
Boron	Chlorine	Nitrogen
D	E	F
Phosphorus	Sodium	Sulphur

(a)   Identify the element which exists as a covalent network solid.

(b)   Identify the **two** elements which exist as discrete covalent molecular solids.

(c)   Identify the **two** elements which react to form the compound with the most ionic character.

45.   There are different families of oxygen-containing carbon compounds.

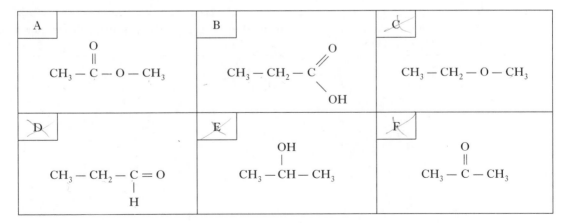

Propan-1-ol is a primary alcohol.

(a)   Identify the **two** isomers of propan-1-ol.

(b)   Identify the compound(s) which could be formed by the oxidation of propan-1-ol.

46. The last five isotopes in a natural radioactive decay series are shown.

$$^{215}Po \rightarrow \ ^{211}Pb \rightarrow \ ^{211}Bi \rightarrow \ ^{207}Tl \rightarrow \ ^{207}Pb$$

Identify the **true** statement(s).

A	^{207}Tl and ^{207}Pb have the same atomic number.
B	^{211}Pb and ^{207}Pb have the same electron arrangement.
C	When ^{215}Po undergoes α-emission, the immediate product is ^{211}Bi.
D	^{211}Pb and ^{211}Bi are isotopes.
E	The nucleus of a ^{215}Po isotope contains 135 neutrons.
F	When ^{207}Tl undergoes β-emission, the immediate product is ^{207}Pb.

47. Metals can be obtained at the negative electrode during electrolysis of molten salts.
Identify the **true** statement(s).

A	Two moles of electrons are required to produce 20 g of calcium.
B	The quantity of electricity required to produce 27 g of aluminium and 23 g of sodium is the same.
C	$2 \cdot 0 \times 10^{23}$ electrons are required to produce 3 g of aluminium.
D	96 500 coulombs are required to produce 80 g of calcium.
E	The quantity of electricity required to produce 40 g of calcium is twice that required to produce 23 g of sodium.

48. A vanadium(V) oxide catalyst is used in the production of sulphur trioxide.

$$SO_2(g) + \tfrac{1}{2}O_2(g) \rightleftharpoons SO_3(g)$$

The potential energy diagram for the uncatalysed reaction is shown.

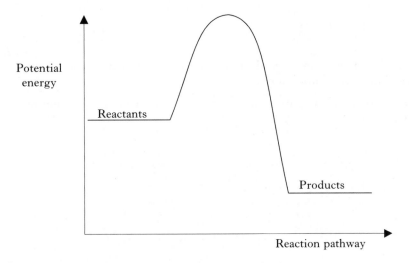

Identify the **true** statement(s).

A	The enthalpy change for the forward reaction is positive.
B	At equilibrium, the energy of activation for the forward reaction is equal to the energy of activation for the reverse reaction.
C	The catalyst decreases the enthalpy change of the reaction.
D	Increasing the pressure increases the yield of sulphur trioxide.
E	The enthalpy change in the forward reaction represents the enthalpy of formation of sulphur trioxide.
F	The catalyst increases the rate of the reverse reaction.

[END OF QUESTION PAPER]

SCOTTISH
CERTIFICATE OF
EDUCATION
1996

WEDNESDAY, 15 MAY
9.30 AM – 12.00 NOON

CHEMISTRY
HIGHER GRADE
Paper II

Marks

1. When samples of elements are placed in the mass spectrometer, the charts obtained provide important information.

   (*a*) The relative atomic mass of iron can be calculated from the information in the following chart.

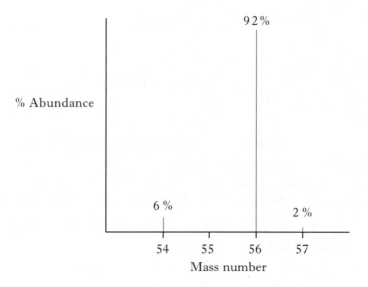

   Calculate the relative atomic mass of iron.

   (Show your working clearly.)

   $$(0.06 \times 54) + (0.92 \times 56) + (0.02 \times 57)$$

   $$=$$

2

Marks

(b) Polonium-218 is an α-emitting radioisotope. The following chart is for a sample which is six minutes old. The half-life of the sample can be found from the chart.

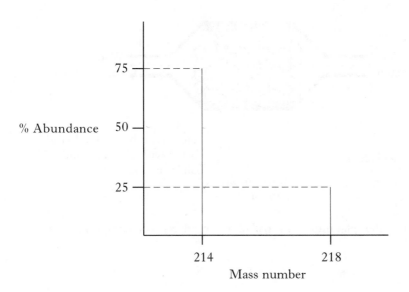

(i) Write a balanced nuclear equation to show the decay of polonium-218.

$$^{218}_{84}Po \longrightarrow ^{214}_{82}Pb + ^{4}_{2}He$$

1

(ii) What is meant by the half-life of the radioisotope?

The time taken for a substance to fall to half its original value

1

(iii) Calculate the half-life of the radioisotope.

1

(5)

Marks

2. Catalysts are an important part of everyday-life.

(*a*) Catalytic convertors are fitted in the exhaust systems of modern cars. These cars use unleaded petrol.

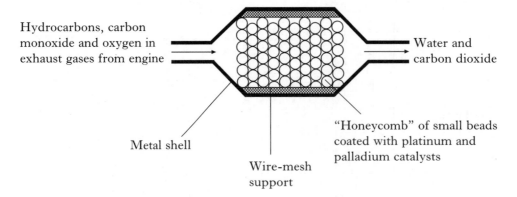

Hydrocarbons, carbon monoxide and oxygen in exhaust gases from engine

Water and carbon dioxide

"Honeycomb" of small beads coated with platinum and palladium catalysts

Metal shell

Wire-mesh support

(i) Why are the platinum and palladium catalysts coated on to small beads?

1

(ii) How would the use of leaded petrol affect the catalyst?

It would use up the active sites and poison the catalyst.

1

(iii) Explain what happens to the molecules in the gas from the engine during the catalytic conversion to water and carbon dioxide.

You may wish to draw labelled diagrams.

2

(*b*) Enzymes are biological catalysts.

(i) Use labelled diagrams to show why an enzyme can only catalyse a specific reaction.

enzyme specific

1

(ii) State **one** factor which can affect the efficiency of an enzyme.

temperature

1

(6)

Marks

3. The graph shows the concentrations of reactant and product as equilibrium is established in a reaction.

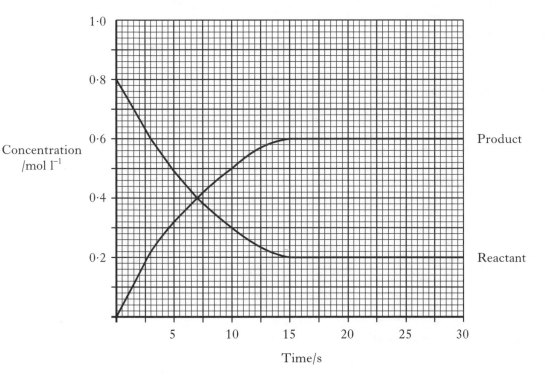

Time/s

(a) Calculate the average rate of reaction over the first 10 s.
(Show your working clearly.)

$0.8 - 0.3 = 0.5$

$\frac{0.5}{10} =$ $mol^{-1}s^{-1}$

1

(b) The equilibrium constant for a reaction is given the symbol **K**. In this reaction **K** is given by:

$$K = \frac{\text{equilibrium concentration of product}}{\text{equilibrium concentration of reactant}}$$

Calculate the value of **K** for this reaction.

1

(c) The reaction is repeated using a homogeneous catalyst.

(i) What is meant by a **homogeneous** catalyst?

It is the same state as the reactants.

1

(ii) What effect would the introduction of the catalyst have on the value of **K**?

Speeds up the reaching of equilibrium.

Has no effect on position

1

(4)

51

Marks

4. The chemical industry uses methane as a feedstock in the production of methanal.

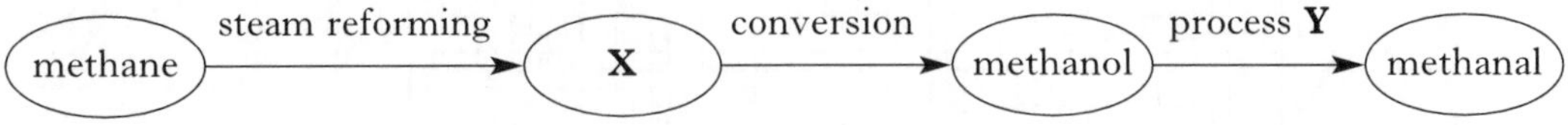

methane —steam reforming→ **X** —conversion→ methanol —process **Y**→ methanal

(*a*) Draw the full structural formula for methanal.

1

(*b*) Name gas mixture **X**.

1

(*c*) Name process **Y**.

1

(*d*) Give an industrial use for methanal.

1

(4)

5. Aluminium oxide, aluminium chloride and aluminium sulphate are three compounds of aluminium.

(*a*) Aluminium oxide is an amphoteric oxide.
What is meant by an amphoteric oxide?

1

(*b*) Aluminium chloride can be hydrolysed.
Name the gas produced in this reaction.

1

(*c*) Aluminium sulphate has the formula $Al_2(SO_4)_3$.
Calculate the number of aluminium ions in $3 \cdot 42$ g of aluminium sulphate.

2

(4)

Marks

6. Butan-2-ol reacts in different ways.

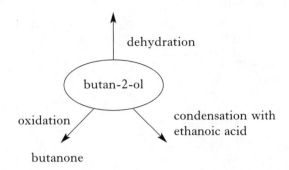

(*a*)   Name the **two** products formed by the dehydration of butan-2-ol.

1

(*b*)   Name a reagent which could be used to oxidise butan-2-ol to butanone.

1

(*c*)   Draw the full structural formula for the ester produced by the condensation of butan-2-ol with ethanoic acid.

1

(3)

Marks

7. A pupil used a cylinder of camping gas to measure the enthalpy of combustion of butane. The experimental set-up is shown.

Aluminium pot containing water

BUTANE

The pupil found that 2·8 g of butane burned to give out 72·4 kJ of energy.

(a) Write a balanced equation to show the reaction which corresponds to the enthalpy of combustion of butane.

1

(b) Apart from the mass of the butane cylinder at the start and the end of the experiment, state **three** measurements which the pupil would have made.

2

(c) Calculate the experimental value for the enthalpy of combustion of butane. **(Show your working clearly.)**

1

(4)

8. The American scientist Linus Pauling devised a scale to compare the attraction of atoms for bonded electrons. This scale is called the electronegativity scale. Some electronegativity values are shown on page 12 of the data booklet.

(a) Which group of the Periodic Table contains elements with no quoted values for electronegativity?

1

(b) Use the electronegativity values to explain why carbon disulphide contains pure covalent bonds.

1

(c) Explain the trend in the electronegativity values of the Group 7 elements.

2

(4)

9. In some countries, cow dung is fermented and the mixture of gases produced, *Marks* known as biogas, is used as a fuel. The mixture contains a small amount of carbon dioxide.

(*a*) Name the main component of the biogas mixture.

1

(*b*) The percentage of carbon dioxide in a biogas sample can be estimated by experiment. Part of the apparatus is shown in the diagram.

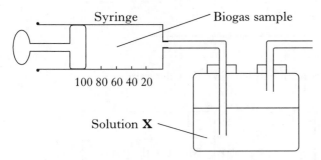

(i) Solution **X** is used to absorb the carbon dioxide.

Give a name for solution **X**.

1

(ii) Complete the diagram to show all of the apparatus which could be used to carry out the experiment.

1

(*c*) Name **one** other fuel which can be made by fermentation.

1

(4)

Marks

10. A pupil is asked to investigate the relationship between the pH of solutions of hydrochloric acid and the concentration of the hydrogen ions when the acid is repeatedly diluted.

(*a*)   (i) Complete this table to show the result of the first dilution.

Concentration of		pH
acid/mol l^{-1}	H^+ions/mol l^{-1}	
1	1	0
0·1	0·1	

1

(ii) Instructions for the experiment are given in a flow diagram.

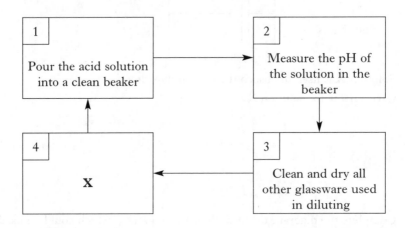

Describe in detail what the pupil should do at the stage marked **X**.

The description should include the volumes and the names of the apparatus used.

3

(*b*) Calculate the concentration of hydroxide ions in a solution of hydrochloric acid with a concentration of 0·001 mol l^{-1}.

1

(5)

Marks

11. Soda water is made by dissolving carbon dioxide in water, under pressure.

$$CO_2(g) + aq \rightleftharpoons CO_2(aq)$$

(*a*) When the stopper is taken off a bottle of soda water, the carbon dioxide gas escapes. Explain why the drink eventually goes **completely** flat.

2

(*b*) This graph shows the solubility of carbon dioxide in water at different temperatures.

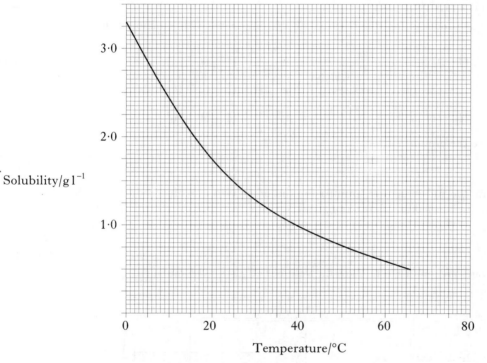

What does the graph indicate about the enthalpy of solution of carbon dioxide in water?

1

(*c*) When all of the carbon dioxide is removed from one litre of soda water at 0 °C, the gas is found to occupy 1·7 litres.

Use information in the graph to calculate the molar volume of carbon dioxide at this temperature.

(Show your working clearly.)

2

(5)

Marks

12. The compound diazomethane, CH_2N_2, undergoes an unusual reaction called **insertion**. Under certain experimental conditions, the CH_2 group produced can insert itself into **any** bond which includes an atom of hydrogen.

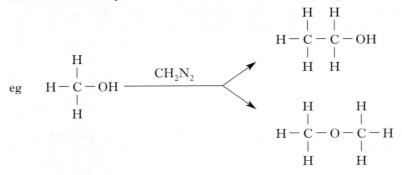

Nitrogen is a product in every reaction.

One of the products for the reaction of diazomethane with ethanol is shown below.

$$
\begin{array}{ccc}
\text{H} & \text{H} & \\
| & | & \\
\text{H}-\text{C}-\text{C}-\text{OH} & & \\
| & | & \\
\text{H} & \text{H} &
\end{array}
\quad \xrightarrow{\;CH_2N_2\;}\quad
\begin{array}{cccc}
\text{H} & \text{H} & \text{H} & \\
| & | & | & \\
\text{H}-\text{C}-\text{C}-\text{C}-\text{OH} & & & \\
| & | & | & \\
\text{H} & \text{H} & \text{H} &
\end{array}
$$

(a) Name the product shown.

1

(b) Draw the full structural formula for the other **two** organic products which could be formed in this reaction.

2

(3)

13. Gas syringes are graduated to allow the volumes of gases to be measured.

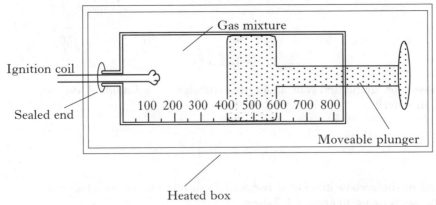

Heated box

The heated box kept the syringe at a temperature greater than 100°C. The syringe contained $150 \, cm^3$ of hydrogen and $50 \, cm^3$ of carbon monoxide mixed with $200 \, cm^3$ of oxygen. When ignited, the gases reacted as shown.

$$CO(g) + 3H_2(g) + 2O_2(g) \longrightarrow CO_2(g) + 3H_2O(g)$$

(a) Name the reactant gas which was in excess and give the remaining volume of this gas.

1

Marks

(*b*) What was the volume and composition of the products of the reaction?

1

(*c*) What would have been the reading on the gas syringe if, at the end of the reaction, the gases had been allowed to cool to room temperature?

1

(3)

14. (*a*) A pupil was investigating the effect of temperature on the rate of reaction. A reaction which produces sulphur and sulphur dioxide from dilute hydrochloric acid and sodium thiosulphate solution was used.

$$Na_2S_2O_3(aq) + 2HCl(aq) \longrightarrow 2NaCl(aq) + SO_2(g) + S(s) + H_2O\ (\ell)$$

This is what was done.

1. The following solutions were measured out.

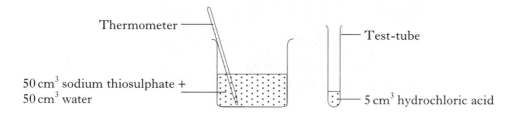

Thermometer

Test-tube

50 cm³ sodium thiosulphate + 50 cm³ water

5 cm³ hydrochloric acid

2. The beaker was heated in a water bath to approximately 30 °C.

3. The beaker was then placed on a card with an **X** on it and the exact temperature of the sodium thiosulphate solution noted.

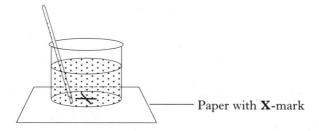

Paper with **X**-mark

4. The acid was added to the sodium thiosulphate solution and the time for the **X** to be obscured by the sulphur formed was noted.

5. The apparatus was thoroughly washed out.

6. The experiment was repeated once at a temperature of approximately 40 °C.

State **three** ways of improving the above investigation procedure.

3

(b) The graph below shows the effect of variation in the concentration of sodium thiosulphate solution when it reacts with hydrochloric acid.

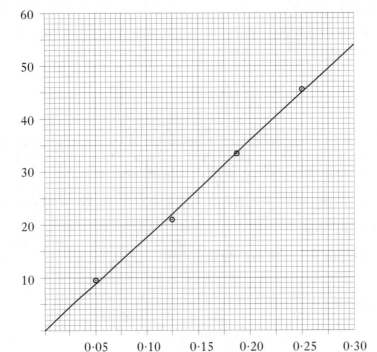

Reaction rate $\left(\dfrac{1}{t}\right) \times 10^3 / \text{s}^{-1}$

Concentration of thiosulphate/mol l^{-1}

(i) One of the reactions was completed in 55·9 seconds.

What concentration of sodium thiosulphate solution was used in this reaction?

(Show your working clearly.)

1

(ii) Why does increasing the concentration result in an increase in the reaction rate?

1

(5)

Marks

15. Ionisation energies can be found by applying an increasing voltage across test samples of gases until the gases ionise.

The results below were obtained from experiments using hydrogen atoms and then helium atoms.

Element	Voltage at which an atom of gas ionises/V	
hydrogen	13·6	no further change
helium	24·6	54·5

(a) Why are there two results for helium but only one for hydrogen?

Hydrogen only has one outer electron, while helium has two.

1

(b) (i) Write an equation which would represent the first ionisation energy of helium gas.

$$He(g) \longrightarrow He^+(g) + e^-$$

1

(ii) Why is the first ionisation energy of helium higher than that of hydrogen?

It has a higher nuclear charge.

1

(c) The ionisation energy, I.E., can be found from:

I.E. = voltage $\times$ 1·6 $\times$ 10^{-19} J

Calculate a value for the first ionisation energy of helium.

(Show your working clearly.)

$$IE = 24.6 \times (1.6 \times 10^{-19})$$
$$IE = 3.936 \times 10^{-18} \ KJ \ mol^{-1}$$

2

(5)

Marks

16. The Group 5 hydrides are covalent compounds.

Compound	Enthalpy of formation/kJ mol^{-1}	Boiling point/K
NH_3	−46	240
PH_3	+6	185
AsH_3	+172	218

(*a*) What is the trend in the stability of the Group 5 hydrides?

There enthalpies of formation increase going down a group.

1

(*b*) Explain why the boiling point of NH_3 is higher than the boiling point of PH_3 and AsH_3.

NH₃ has hydrogen bonding while PH₃ and AsH₃ don't.
Harder bonds to overcome so boiling point is higher.

2

(*c*) The mean bond enthalpy of the P–H bond in $PH_3(g)$ can be found by using the enthalpy change represented by the equation:

$$P(g) \; + \; 3H(g) \; \rightarrow \; PH_3(g)$$

The enthalpy of sublimation of phosphorus is $315 \, kJ \, mol^{-1}$;

the enthalpy of formation of phosphorus hydride is given in the table at the top of the page;

the H–H bond enthalpy is given in the data booklet.

Write equations to represent each of the above enthalpy changes and hence calculate the mean bond enthalpy of the P–H bond.

3

(6)

Marks

17. Terephthallic acid is a commercially important molecule.

The feedstock is p-xylene and three simple reactions are involved in the production process.

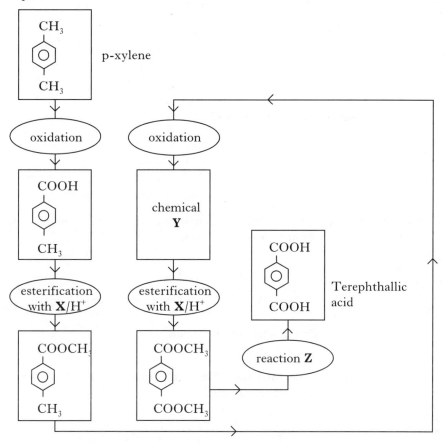

(*a*)   (i) Give the systematic name for p-xylene.

1,4 - dimethylbenzene

1

(ii) Name the oil fraction likely to provide the source of p-xylene.

naphtha

1

(iii) Name the chemical **X** used in the esterification.

methanol

1

Marks

(iv) Draw a structural formula for chemical **Y**.

1

(v) What name is given to reaction **Z**?

1

(b) Terephthallic acid is used in the production of terylene. Terylene is a linear textile fibre commonly known as a polyester.

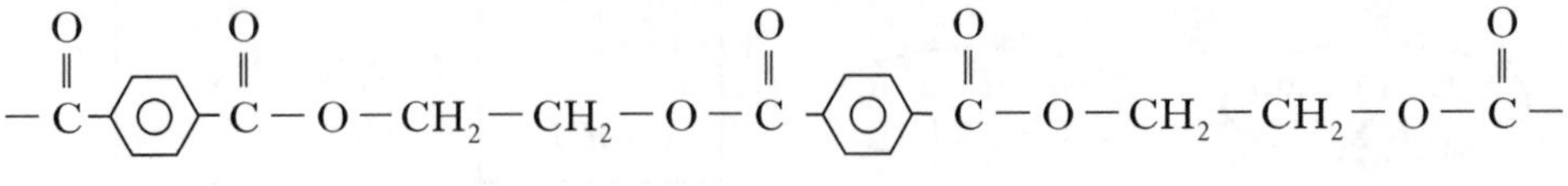

$$-\overset{O}{\overset{\|}{C}}-\langle O \rangle -\overset{O}{\overset{\|}{C}}-O-CH_2-CH_2-O-\overset{O}{\overset{\|}{C}}-\langle O \rangle -\overset{O}{\overset{\|}{C}}-O-CH_2-CH_2-O-\overset{O}{\overset{\|}{C}}-$$

Part of a terylene molecule

(i) What type of polymerisation has taken place in the formation of terylene from terephthallic acid?

condensation

1

(ii) Draw the full structural formula for the other monomer used in terylene manufacture.

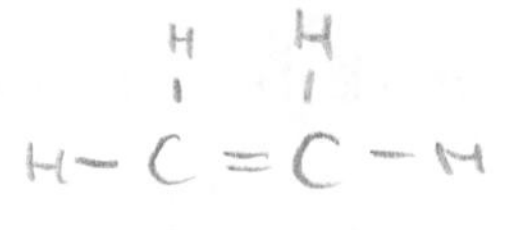

$$H-C=C-H$$
with H H above the two carbons

1

(iii) How would the structure of a cured polyester **resin** differ from the structure of a linear polyester?

1

(8)

Marks

18. The purity of iron(II) salts can be found by titration with acidified potassium permanganate solution.

Equations:

$$Fe^{2+}(aq) \rightarrow Fe^{3+}(aq) + e$$

$$MnO_4^-(aq) + 8H^+(aq) + 5e \rightarrow Mn^{2+}(aq) + 4H_2O\ (\ell)$$

(*a*) This reaction can be described as self-indicating.

How can the end-point be detected?

when it turns slightly purple.

1

(*b*) A pupil was given $1.55\,g$ of impure iron(II) sulphate, $FeSO_4.7H_2O$, and used this to prepare $250\,cm^3$ of solution for the titration.

It was found that $9.5\,cm^3$ of $0.01\,mol\,l^{-1}$ acidified potassium permanganate solution was required to oxidise $25\,cm^3$ of the iron(II) sulphate solution.

(i) Use this information to show that the $250\,cm^3$ solution contained 4.75×10^{-3} mol of iron(II) sulphate.

(Show your working clearly.)

2

(ii) The percentage purity of a salt can be found from the relationship:

$$\text{Percentage purity} = \frac{\text{mass of pure salt}}{\text{mass of impure salt}} \times 100$$

Calculate the mass of pure iron(II) sulphate and thus find the percentage purity of the iron(II) sulphate salt.

(Show your working clearly.)

2

(5)

Marks

19. Prefixes can be used to indicate the number of atoms in a molecule.

Term	Number of atoms in the molecule	Example
diatomic	2	hydrogen chloride
triatomic	3	carbon dioxide
tetra-atomic	4	sulphur trioxide
penta-atomic	5	tetrachloromethane
hexa-atomic	6	phosphorus pentachloride

(*a*) What term is used to describe the following molecule?

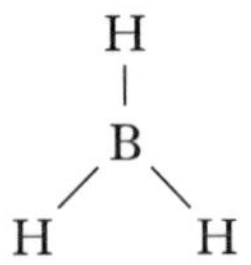

tetra-atomic

1

(*b*) Name a hexa-atomic molecule, containing carbon, which will decolourise bromine water rapidly.

cyclo

1

(*c*) Write the formula for a carbon compound consisting of penta-atomic molecules with a molecular mass of 85.

1

(3)

Marks

20. The idea of **oxidation number** leads to a systematic method of naming inorganic compounds.

The systematic name of $KClO_3$ is potassium chlorate(V) where the Roman numeral in brackets represents the oxidation number of the chlorine atom.

Simplified rules for working out oxidation numbers are:

all Group 1 metals have an oxidation number of +1;

oxygen has an oxidation number of −2;

the sum of the oxidation numbers of all atoms in the formula of a compound is zero.

(*a*) Complete the table below.

Formula	Oxidation number of non-oxygen atom in the negative ion	Systematic name	Charge on the negative ion
$KClO_3$	+5	potassium chlorate(V)	−1
Na_2SO_4	+6	sodium sulphate(I)	−2
	+7	potassium iodate(VII)	−1
Na_3PO_4			

2

(*b*) In acid solution, potassium chlorate(V), $KClO_3(aq)$, oxidises sodium iodide.

   (i) Write an ion-electron equation for the oxidation reaction.

1

   (ii) During the reaction, chlorate(V) ions are reduced to form chlorine.

$$ClO_3^- \quad \rightarrow \quad Cl_2$$

Complete the above to form the ion-electron equation.

1

(4)

[END OF QUESTION PAPER]

SCOTTISH
CERTIFICATE OF
EDUCATION
1997

MONDAY, 19 MAY
1.00 PM – 2.40 PM

CHEMISTRY
HIGHER GRADE
Paper I

PART 1

1. Which is a non-conductor but becomes a good conductor on melting?

   A Solid potassium fluoride

   B Solid argon ✗

   C Solid potassium

   D Solid tetrachloromethane ✗

2. Barium chloride solution would **not** give a precipitate with a solution of a

   A carbonate

   B sulphate

   C sulphite

   D nitrate.

3. $20\,cm^3$ of $0.3\,mol\,l^{-1}$ sodium hydroxide solution can be exactly neutralised by

   A $20\,cm^3\ 0.3\,mol\,l^{-1}$ sulphuric acid H

   B $20\,cm^3\ 0.6\,mol\,l^{-1}$ sulphuric acid

   C $10\,cm^3\ 0.6\,mol\,l^{-1}$ sulphuric acid

   D $10\,cm^3\ 0.3\,mol\,l^{-1}$ sulphuric acid.

4. 56 g of an oxide of lead was strongly heated and hydrogen gas was passed over it. When the oxide was completely reduced, 52 g of lead remained.

   A possible formula for the oxide is

   A Pb_2O_3

   B PbO_2

   C Pb_2O

   D PbO.

5. A mixture of magnesium bromide and magnesium sulphate is known to contain 3 mol of magnesium and 4 mol of bromide ions.

   How many moles of sulphate ions are present?

   A 1

   B 2

   C 3

   D 4

6. The following potential energy diagram represents the energy changes in a chemical reaction.

   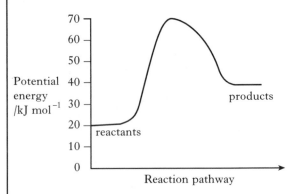

   The activation energy for the reaction, in $kJ\,mol^{-1}$, is

   A 20

   B 30

   C 50

   D 70.

7. Which of the following is not a correct statement about the effect of a catalyst?

   The catalyst

   A provides an alternative route to the products

   B lowers the energy which molecules need for successful collisions

   C provides energy so that more molecules have successful collisions

   D forms bonds with reacting molecules.

8. The graph shows the volume of hydrogen given off against time when an excess of magnesium ribbon is added to $100\,cm^3$ of hydrochloric acid (concentration $1\ mol\,l^{-1}$) at $20\,°C$.

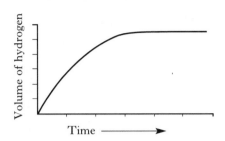

Which graph would show the volume of hydrogen given off when an excess of magnesium ribbon is added to $50\,cm^3$ of hydrochloric acid of the same concentration at $30\,°C$?

A

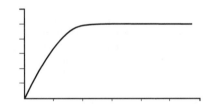

B

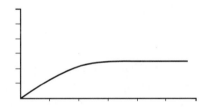

C

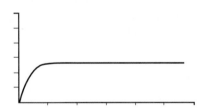

D

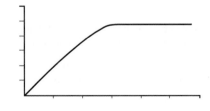

9.

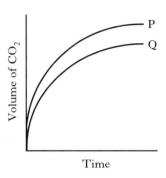

When copper carbonate is reacted with excess acid, carbon dioxide is produced. The curves shown above were obtained under different conditions.

The change from P to Q could be brought about by

A increasing the concentration of the acid

B decreasing the mass of copper carbonate

C decreasing the particle size of the copper carbonate

D adding a catalyst.

10.

$$CH_3 - \underset{\underset{H}{|}}{\overset{\overset{CH_3}{|}}{C}} - CH_2 - \underset{\underset{H}{|}}{\overset{\overset{OH}{|}}{C}} - CH_3$$

The product of oxidation of the above structure is

A 4-methylpentan-2-one

B 2-methylpentan-4-one

C 2-methylpentanal

D 4-methylpentanal.

11. When ethanol is passed over heated aluminium oxide, the main product will be

A ethane

B ethene

C ethanal

D ethanoic acid.

12. A compound used in the synthesis of thermosetting plastics is:

The name of this compound is

A methanol

B methanal

C methanoic acid

D methanone.

13. The tendency of a petrol component to ignite spontaneously is measured by its octane number.

	Compound	Octane number
1	3-methylpentane	74·5
2	pentane	61·7
3	butane	93·6
4	2-methylpentane	73·4
5	hexane	24·8
6	methylcyclopentane	91·3

A pupil made the hypothesis that as the chain length of a hydrocarbon increases, the octane number decreases.

Which set of 3 components should have their octane numbers compared in order to test this hypothesis?

A 1, 4, 6

B 1, 2, 4

C 2, 3, 5

D 3, 4, 5

14. In nature, carbon is continually being recycled. Part of the cycle is shown below.

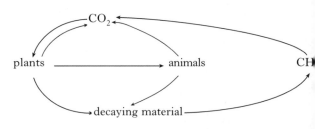

The production of methane from decaying material is due to

A photosynthesis

B respiration

C aerobic fermentation

D anaerobic fermentation.

15. Using the density quoted in the Data Booklet, what is the number of moles of nitrogen molecules in a 5 litre container?

A 0·11

B 0·21

C 0·31

D 0·41

16. $3CuO + 2NH_3 \rightarrow 3Cu + N_2 + 3H_2O$

What volume of gas, in cm^3, would be obtained by reaction between $100\,cm^3$ of ammonia gas and excess copper(II) oxide?

(All volumes are measured at atmospheric pressure and $20\,°C$.)

A 50

B 100

C 200

D 400

17. Diabetics suffer from a deficiency of the protein insulin (formula mass 6000).

What mass of insulin will contain approximately 3×10^{20} molecules?

A 3 g

B 6 g

C 30 g

D 60 g

18. If 96 500 C of electricity are passed through separate solutions of copper(II) chloride and nickel(II) chloride, then

A equal masses of copper and nickel will be deposited

B the same number of atoms of each metal will be deposited

C the metals will be plated on the positive electrode

D different numbers of moles of each metal will be deposited.

19. During a redox process in acid solution, iodate ions, $IO_3^-(aq)$, are converted into iodine, $I_2(aq)$.

$$IO_3^-(aq) \rightarrow I_2(aq)$$

The numbers of $H^+(aq)$ and $H_2O(\ell)$ required to balance the ion-electron equation for the formation of 1 mol of $I_2(aq)$ are, respectively

A 6 and 3

B 3 and 6

C 12 and 6

D 6 and 12.

20. Ethyl butanoate is used in pineapple flavouring.

The formulae for the molecules from which it is made are

A C_3H_7OH and CH_3COOH

B C_2H_5OH and C_2H_5COOH

C C_3H_7COOH and C_2H_5OH

D C_2H_5COOH and C_3H_7OH.

21. The monomer units used to construct enzyme molecules are

A esters

B amino acids

C fatty acids

D monosaccharides.

22. Polyester fibres and cured polyester are both very strong.

What kinds of structure do their molecules have?

	Fibre	Cured resin
A	cross-linked	cross-linked
B	linear	linear
C	cross-linked	linear
D	linear	cross-linked

23. Graphite, a form of carbon, conducts electricity because it has

A metallic bonding

B van der Waals bonding

C delocalised electrons

D pure covalent bonding.

24. Which type of bonding can be described as intermolecular?

A Covalent

B Hydrogen

C Ionic

D Metallic

25. Which chloride is most likely to be soluble in tetrachloromethane, CCl_4?

A Barium chloride

B Caesium chloride

C Calcium chloride

D Phosphorus chloride

26. On descending the halogen group of the Periodic Table, the

A attracting power for bonding electrons increases

B ionisation energy increases

C nuclear charge increases

D reactivity increases.

27. Which of the following compounds has polar molecules?

    A CH_4

    B CO_2

    C NH_3

    D CCl_4

28. Phosphorus trichloride reacts with water giving a gaseous product. This is most likely to consist of

    A chlorine only

    B hydrogen chloride only

    C a mixture of hydrogen and chlorine

    D a mixture of hydrogen chloride and chlorine.

29. Which process is exothermic?

    A $Li^+(g) \rightarrow Li^+(aq)$

    B $Li(s) \rightarrow Li(g)$

    C $Li(g) \rightarrow Li^+(g)$

    D $Li(s) \rightarrow Li(\ell)$

30. In which of the following reactions would the energy change represent the lattice enthalpy of sodium chloride?

    A $Na^+(g) + Cl^-(g) \rightarrow NaCl(s)$

    B $Na(g) + Cl(g) \rightarrow NaCl(s)$

    C $Na(s) + \frac{1}{2}Cl_2(g) \rightarrow NaCl(s)$

    D $Na(s) + Cl(g) \rightarrow NaCl(s)$

31. In the presence of bright light, hydrogen and chlorine react explosively. One step in the reaction is shown below.

$H_2(g) + Cl(g) \rightarrow HCl(g) + H(g)$

The enthalpy change for this step can be represented as the bond enthalpy of

    A $H-H + Cl-Cl$

    B $H-H - Cl-Cl$

    C $H-H + H-Cl$

    D $H-H - H-Cl$

32. Which of these processes can be described as an enthalpy of formation?

    A $C_2H_4(g) + H_2(g) \rightarrow C_2H_6(g)$

    B $2C(s) + 3H_2(g) \rightarrow C_2H_6(g)$

    C $2C(g) + 6H(g) \rightarrow C_2H_6(g)$

    D $C_2H_2(g) + 2H_2(g) \rightarrow C_2H_6(g)$

33. The bond enthalpy of the $N-H$ bond is equal to $\frac{1}{3}$ of the value of ΔH for which change?

    A $N(g) + 3H(g) \rightarrow NH_3(g)$

    B $N_2(g) + 3H_2(g) \rightarrow 2NH_3(g)$

    C $\frac{1}{2}N_2(g) + 1\frac{1}{2}H_2(g) \rightarrow NH_3(g)$

    D $2NH_3(g) + 1\frac{1}{2}O_2(g) \rightarrow N_2(g) + 3H_2O(g)$

34. $ICl(\ell) + Cl_2(g) \rightleftharpoons ICl_3(s)$ $\Delta H = -106$ kJ mol^{-1}

Which of the following sets of changes will cause the greatest increase in the proportion of solid in the above equilibrium?

	Temperature	Pressure
A	decrease	decrease
B	decrease	increase
C	increase	decrease
D	increase	increase

35. A trout fishery owner added limestone to his loch to combat the effects of acid rain. He managed to raise the pH of the water from 4 to 6.

This caused the concentration of the $H^+(aq)$ to

    A increase by a factor of 2

    B increase by a factor of 100

    C decrease by a factor of 2

    D decrease by a factor of 100.

36. A fully dissociated acid is progressively diluted by the addition of water.

Which of the following would increase with increasing dilution?

A   The pH value

B   The electrical conductivity

C   The rate of its reaction with chalk

D   The volume of alkali which it will neutralise

37. A pH value greater than 7 would be shown by a $1 \cdot 0 \, \text{mol} \, l^{-1}$ solution of

A   sodium sulphate

B   ammonium chloride

C   potassium ethanoate

D   lithium chloride.

38. The stability of the nucleus of an ion depends on the ratio of

A   mass : charge

B   neutrons : protons

C   neutrons : electrons

D   protons : electrons.

39. The following represents part of a natural radioactive decay series.

$$^{x}U \xrightarrow{\alpha} \; ^{y}Th \xrightarrow{\beta} \; ^{231}Pa$$

Which of the following represent the mass numbers x and y?

	x	y
A	239	235
B	232	231
C	237	233
D	235	231

40. When some zinc pellets containing radioactive zinc are placed in a solution of zinc chloride, radioactivity soon appears in the solution.

Compared with that of the pellets, the half-life of the radioactive solution will be

A   shorter

B   the same

C   longer

D   dependent upon how long the zinc is in contact with the solution.

PART 2

41. Many organic compounds contain oxygen.

A	B	C
CH$_3$COOH	HCHO	CH$_3$COOCH$_3$

D	E	F
CH$_3$OH	HOCH$_2$CH$_2$OH	(COOH)$_2$

(a) Identify the product of the oxidation of the compound shown in box D.

(b) Identify **two** compounds which could be used to make a polyester.

42.

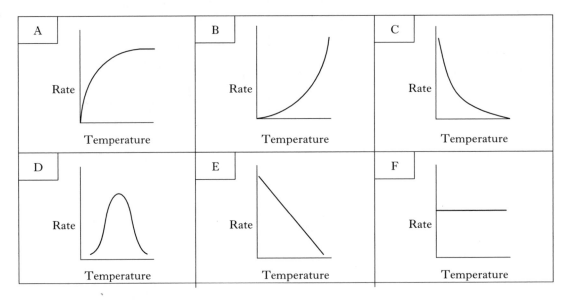

Identify the graph which shows how the rate varies with temperature in

(a) the reaction between sodium thiosulphate solution and dilute hydrochloric acid,

(b) the fermentation of glucose,

(c) the radioactive decay of uranium-235.

43. Hydrocarbons are compounds containing hydrogen and carbon only.

A		B		C	
C_2H_4		C_3H_8		C_4H_{10}	
D		**E**		**F**	
C_4H_8		C_6H_{14}		CH_4	

(a) Identify the hydrocarbon which could belong to two different homologous series.

(b) Identify the hydrocarbon which could be produced by reforming the hydrocarbon shown in box C.

(c) Identify the **two** hydrocarbons which could be produced by cracking the hydrocarbon shown in box B.

44. The first twenty elements can be described in different ways.

A		B		C	
Covalent		Metallic		Made up of discrete molecules	
D		**E**		**F**	
Made up of diatomic molecules		Gas		Solid	

(a) Identify the term which can be applied to lithium but **not** carbon.

(b) Identify the term(s) which can be applied to **both** fluorine and phosphorus.

45. The following solutions have a concentration of 1 mol l^{-1}.

A		B		C	
HCl(aq)		NH$_4$Cl(aq)		NH$_3$(aq)	
D		**E**		**F**	
CH$_3$COOH(aq)		Na$_2$CO$_3$(aq)		NaCl(aq)	

(a)   Identify the solution which contains an equal number of H$^+$(aq) and OH$^-$(aq) ions.

(b)   Identify the solution(s) with a pH greater than 1 but less than 7.

46. Many organic compounds have different isomers.

Identify the compound(s) with isomeric forms.

A		B		C	
CH$_3$CH$_2$CH$_2$Cl		CH$_3$CH$_2$Cl		CH$_2$CHCl	
D		**E**		**F**	
CH$_2$CCl$_2$		CCl$_2$CCl$_2$		CH$_3$Cl	

47. Two flasks contained equal volumes of 0·1 mol l^{-1} hydrochloric acid and 0·1 mol l^{-1} ethanoic acid.
Identify the **true** statement(s) about the two solutions.

A	They give the same colour with Universal indicator.
B	They have pH less than 7.
C	They conduct electricity equally well.
D	They have equal concentrations of hydrogen ions.
E	They react at the same rate with magnesium.
F	They neutralise the same number of moles of sodium hydroxide.

48. An atom of X, a Group 1 element, reacts to become an ion, X^+.

Identify the **true** statement(s) about this change.

A	The diameter of the particle increases.
B	The nucleus acquires a positive charge.
C	The number of energy levels (electron shells) decreases by one.
D	The atomic number increases by one.
E	An electron is emitted from the nucleus.
F	The number of neutrons does not change.

[END OF QUESTION PAPER]

SCOTTISH
CERTIFICATE OF
EDUCATION
1997

MONDAY, 19 MAY
9.30 AM – 12.00 NOON

CHEMISTRY
HIGHER GRADE
Paper II

Marks

1. One of the fractions obtained from crude oil is natural gas liquid, NGL, a mixture of hydrocarbons, which is used as a feedstock for various processes.

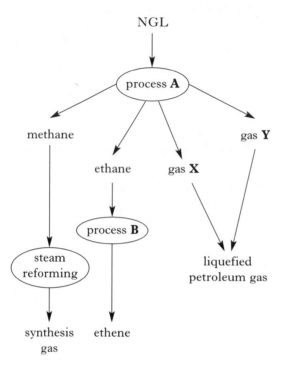

(*a*) Name

    (i) the two main components of synthesis gas,

        carbon monoxide, hydrogen

                                                                        1

    (ii) gas **X** and gas **Y**.

        propane, butane

                                                                        1

(*b*) Name

    (i) process **A**,

        distillation

                                                                        1

    (ii) process **B**.

        cracking

                                                                        1

                                                                           (4)

Marks

2.

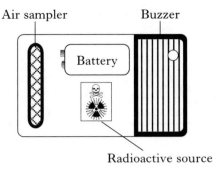

Air sampler   Buzzer

Battery

Radioactive source

Smoke detectors use the alpha radiation from americium-241 to ionise the air in a small chamber. When smoke is present, the conductivity of the air is changed and a buzzer is activated.

(a) Write a balanced nuclear equation for the alpha decay of americium-241.

$$^{241}_{95}Am \longrightarrow \ ^{237}_{93}Np + \ ^{4}_{2}He$$

1

(b) The half-life of americium-241 is 433 years.

Calculate the time taken for the activity of the sample to fall to 12·5% of its original value.

100 % – 0 years
50% – 433 years
25% – 866 years
12·5% – 1299 years

1

(c) Give **two** reasons why americium-241 is a suitable radioisotope for use in an overhead smoke detector.

It has a long half life.

2

(d) A smoke detector uses 10^{-6} g of americium-241.

Calculate the number of atoms in this sample.

1 mol $\rightarrow$ 241g

241g $\rightarrow$ 6·02 × 10^{23}

1g $\rightarrow$ $\dfrac{6·02 × 10^{23}}{241}$

0·000001g $\rightarrow$ $\dfrac{6·02 × 10^{23}}{241}$ × 0·000001

$\Rightarrow$ 2·508 × 10^{15} atoms

2

(6)

Marks

3. Some of the chemistry of Al_2O_3 is shown in the flow chart.

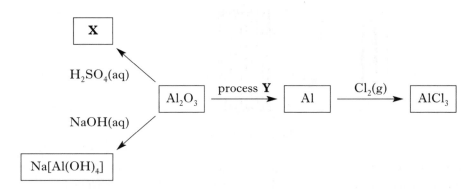

(*a*) What evidence from the chart indicates that Al_2O_3 is amphoteric?

It can react with both an acid and an alkali to give salts.

1

(*b*) Write the formula for salt **X**.

$$Al_2O_3 + 3H_2SO_4 \longrightarrow Al_2(SO_4)_3 + 3H_2O$$

$$Al_2(SO_4)_3$$

1

(*c*) In industry, how is the reduction of Al_2O_3 carried out in process **Y**?

By electrolysis

1

(*d*) $AlCl_3$ cannot be obtained by the reaction of $Al_2O_3(s)$ with $HCl(aq)$.
Why does $AlCl_3$ **not** exist in aqueous solution?

Because $AlCl_3$ is extremely soluble

1

(4)

Marks

4. The following triglyceride is found in some fats and oils.

$$H_2C - O - C - (CH_2)_{16}CH_3$$
$$\underset{O}{\|}$$

$$HC - O - C - (CH_2)_7CH = CH(CH_2)_7CH_3$$
$$\underset{O}{\|}$$

$$H_2C - O - C - (CH_2)_{16}CH_3$$
$$\underset{O}{\|}$$

(a) The triglycerides in fats and oils belong to which type of compound?

, esters

1

(b) The hydrolysis of the triglyceride produces an alcohol and long chain fatty acids.

(i) Name the alcohol produced by the hydrolysis of the triglyceride.

glycerol

1

(ii) Suggest why the sequence of fatty acids in the triglyceride can be referred to as S,O,S.

You may wish to refer to page 6 of the data booklet.

because s is stearic acid and o is oleic acid and they are in the sequence stearic, oleic, stearic

1

(c) What happens to triglyceride molecules in the conversion of oils to hardened fats?

They get hydrogen added to them, so they become saturated.

1

(4)

Marks

5. Chlorofluorocarbons, commonly known as CFCs, are widely used in fridges, aerosols and to preserve blood in blood banks.

(*a*) Information about three CFCs is shown in the table.

CFC	Name	Structure
12	dichlorodifluoromethane	. . . . .
13	1,1,2-trichloro-1,2,2-trifluoroethane	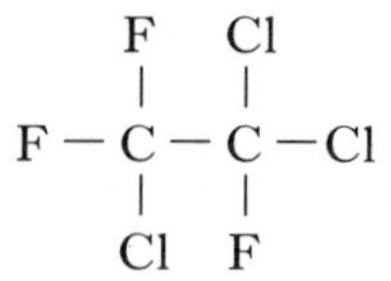 F—C—C—Cl with F, Cl on top and Cl, F on bottom
114	. . . . .	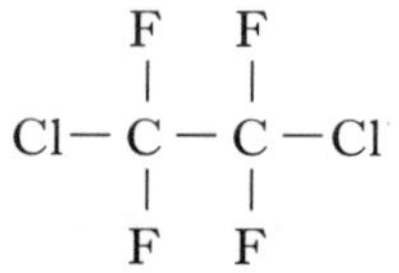 Cl—C—C—Cl with F, F on top and F, F on bottom

(i) Draw the full structural formula for CFC 12.

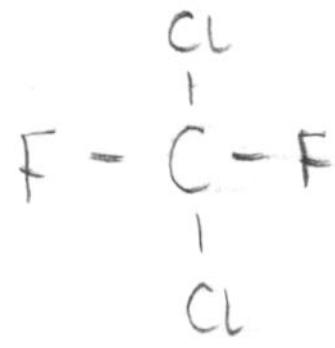

$$F - \overset{\displaystyle Cl}{\underset{\displaystyle Cl}{C}} - F$$

1

(ii) Give the name of CFC 114.

1,2 - dichloro -1,1,2,2 - tetrafluoroethane

1

(b) Concern about the ozone layer has led to the replacement of CFCs by HFAs, compounds which contain hydrogen in addition to carbon, fluorine and chlorine.

Three properties of CFCs and HFAs are linked to the proportion of chlorine, fluorine and hydrogen in their molecules as shown in the diagram.

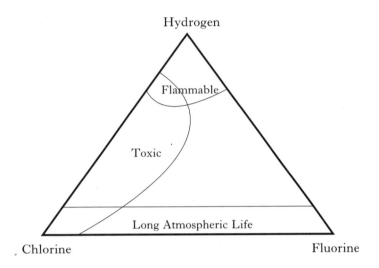

Use the three terms in the diagram to compare the properties of the following two compounds.

Compound	Formula
HFA 134a	CF_3CH_2F
CFC 13	CF_2ClCCl_2F

HFA 134a - has a long atmospheric life
           its flammable

CFC 13 - has a long atmospheric life
       - is toxic
           and flammable

both have long atmospheric lives
    and are flammable, however
    CFC 13 is toxic and HFA 134a isn't

1

(3)

Marks

6. Laundry bags, used in hospitals, are made from poly(ethenol), a polymer which will dissolve in hot or cold water.

Poly(ethenol) is made from a monomer which has the following structure.

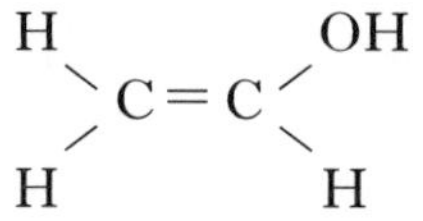

$$\begin{array}{ccc} H & & OH \\ & C=C & \\ H & & H \end{array}$$

(a) What type of polymerisation produces poly(ethenol)?

condensation polymerisation

1

(b) Draw the full structural formula for a section of the polymer made from **three** of these monomer units.

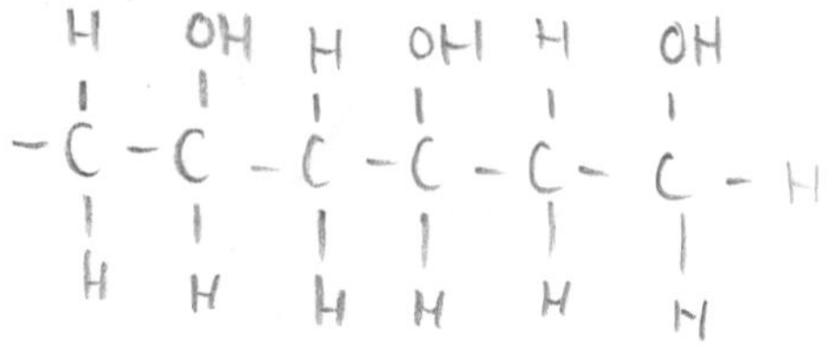

— C — C — C — C — C — C — H
(with H, OH, H, OH, H, OH on top and H, H, H, H, H, H on bottom)

1

(c) Poly(ethene) is insoluble in water.

Explain why poly(ethenol) is soluble in water.

2

(4)

7. The most common method for the industrial purification of gold is the cyanide process.

(a) The impure gold is first dissolved in sodium cyanide solution, NaCN, to give sodium gold cyanide, $NaAu(CN)_2$.

The partially balanced equation for the reaction is:

$$4Au + 8NaCN + O_2 + 2H_2O \longrightarrow 4NaAu(CN)_2 + 4NaOH$$

Complete the balancing of this equation.

1

Marks

(b) The gold is then obtained by a redox reaction using zinc.

$$2NaAu(CN)_2(aq) + Zn(s) \longrightarrow Na_2Zn(CN)_4(aq) + 2Au(s)$$

Give another name for this type of reaction.

displacement

1

(c) Gold may be purified by electrolysis.

(i) In an industrial process, a current of 10 000 A was passed through a gold solution for 25 minutes producing 10·21 kg of gold.

Calculate the charge on the gold ions in the solution.

(Show your working clearly.)

Au
↳ 197

$Q = I \times t$

$Q = I \times (25 \times 60)$

$Q = I \times 1500$

$Q = 10\,000 \times 1500$

$Q = 15,000,000$ C

$15,000,000 \longrightarrow 10,210$ g

$10,210$ g $\longrightarrow 15,000,000$

1 g $\longrightarrow \dfrac{15,000,000}{10,210}$

197 g $\longrightarrow 289,422.1352$ C

1 mol $\longrightarrow 6.02 \times 10^{23}$

197 g $\longrightarrow 6.02 \times 10^{23}$

$1 \longrightarrow \dfrac{6.02 \times 10^{23}}{197}$

$1 \longrightarrow 3.0558 \times 10^{21}$

(ii) In the laboratory, the electrolysis of gold chloride solution can be used to find the number of coulombs required to plate 1 g of gold on pure gold sheet. The second electrode would be impure gold.

Draw a clearly labelled diagram of the assembled apparatus.

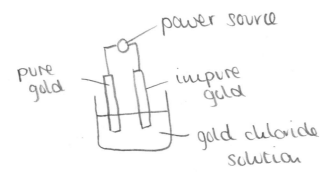

power source

pure gold

impure gold

gold chloride solution

2

(7)

Marks

8. Urea is a substance found in human urine. The enzyme urease catalyses the hydrolysis of urea.

$$CO(NH_2)_2 + H_2O \xrightarrow{\text{urease enzyme}} CO_2 + 2NH_3$$
urea

The concentration of urea in a sample can be estimated using an indicator as shown in the diagram.

— Urea sample
— Urease extract

— Acidified gel
+
Bromothymol blue indicator

The bromothymol blue indicator is yellow below pH 6 and blue above pH 8·3.

(a) Draw the full structural formula for urea.

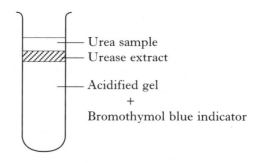

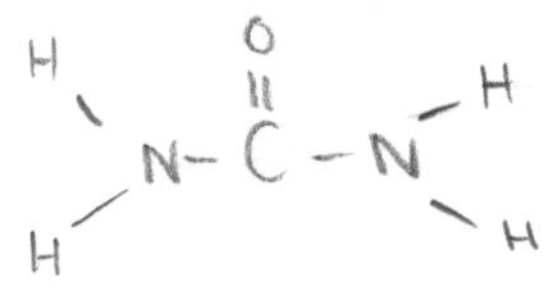

1

(b) The initial yellow colour of the indicator changed to blue as the experiment proceeded.

Explain **fully** the colours observed.

becoming more alkali so there is more NH_3 being made, so urea is being broken down constantly by urease.

2

Marks

(c)   The pH of the gel after one completed experiment was found to be 11.

Calculate the concentration of hydroxide ions.

$$[H^+][OH^-] = 10^{-14}$$
$$[OH^-] = 10^{-14} \div [H^+]$$
$$= 10^{-14} \div 10^{-11}$$
$$[OH^-] = 10^{-3}$$

$$pH = 11$$
$$pH = -\log(10^{-11})$$

1

(d)   The graph shows the potential energy diagram for a urease catalysis of urea.

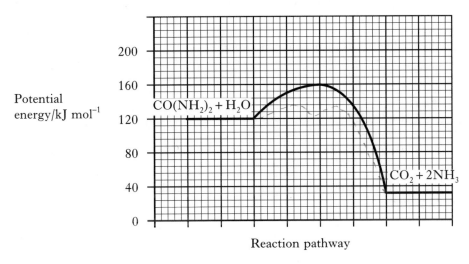

Reaction pathway

(i)   What is the enthalpy change for the reaction?

The enthalpy change is $\Delta H = H_p - H_r$
$\Delta H = 32 - 120$ $\Delta H = -88 \, KJ \, mol^{-1}$

1

(ii) Acid is a **less** effective catalyst than urease for this reaction.

Add a curve to the potential energy diagram to show the hydrolysis when acid is used as the catalyst.

1

(6)

Marks

9. Graph 1 shows the boiling points of the Group 7 elements.

Graph 1

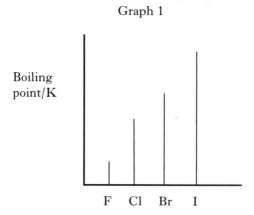

(a) Why do the boiling points increase down Group 7?

   Because the Van der Waals increases
   because there is more electrons which
   causes a bigger 'wobble' so therefore,
   large attractions.

1

(b) Graph 2 shows the melting points of elements from lithium to neon across the second period.

Graph 2

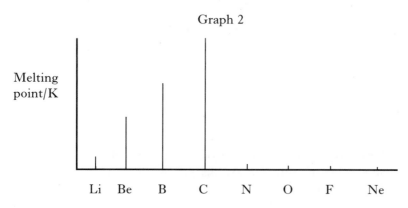

Give a reason for the high melting points of boron and carbon.

   They are covalent networks, have
      strong covalent bonds throughout.

1

Marks

(c) Graph 3 shows the first ionisation energies of the Group 1 elements.

Graph 3

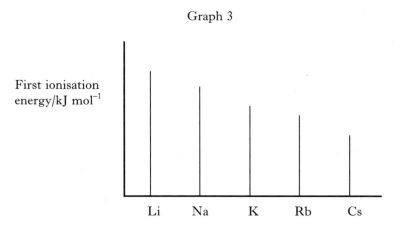

First ionisation
energy/kJ mol^{-1}

Li   Na   K   Rb   Cs

Explain why there is a decrease in first ionisation energy down this group.

*Because there is an increase in energy
levels, so the outer electrons are further away
from the nucleus so less energy is required
to remove electrons.*

2

(d) Graph 4 shows the first ionisation energies of successive elements with increasing atomic number.

Graph 4

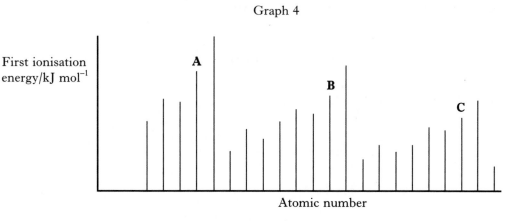

First ionisation
energy/kJ mol^{-1}

A

B

C

Atomic number

Elements **A**, **B** and **C** belong to the same group of the Periodic Table.
Identify the group.

Group 5

1

(5)

Marks

10. Lactic acid can be found in wine. The acid contains both the hydroxyl and the carboxyl functional groups.

$$CH_3 - CH - COOH \qquad \text{lactic}$$
$$\underset{\text{(OH)}}{|} \qquad \qquad \text{acid}$$

(a) Circle the hydrogen atom of the above lactic acid molecule which would be replaced in the reaction of lactic acid with magnesium.

1

(b) Name the substance **X** which reacts with lactic acid in the following equation.

$$CH_3 - CH - COOH \quad + \quad 2\mathbf{X} \quad \longrightarrow \quad CH_3 - CH - COONa \quad + \quad H_2$$
$$\underset{OH}{|} \qquad \qquad \qquad \qquad \underset{ONa}{|}$$

Na - sodium

1

(c) Name the substance which reacts with lactic acid to produce the following compound.

$$CH_3 - CH - COONa$$
$$\underset{OH}{|}$$

sodium hydride

1

(d) The following compound is sometimes found in wine.

$$CH_3 - CH - COOCH_2CH_3$$
$$\underset{OH}{|}$$

Explain why this compound can be formed.

it is formed when an acid is oxidised

2

(5)

Marks

11. A pupil tried to confirm Hess's Law using the reactions shown below.

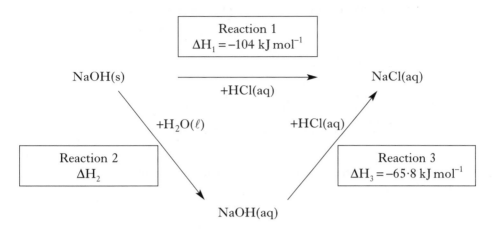

In reaction 1, the pupil measured the mass of NaOH(s) and the temperature change of the reaction mixture.

(*a*) Which further measurement would have been taken?

The mass of NaCl(aq)

1

(*b*) Use the enthalpy changes in the diagram to calculate the enthalpy change for reaction 2.

$\Delta H_1 = \Delta H_2 + \Delta H_3$

$-104 = \Delta H_2 + -65.8$

$-104 + 65.8 = \Delta H_2$

$\Delta H_2 = -38.2 \text{ KJmol}^{-1}$

1

(*c*) Write, in words, a statement of Hess's Law.

Hess's Law states that no matter which pathway you take from reactants to products, the enthalpy change is always the same

1

(3)

Marks

12. Synthetic perfumes are cheaper and easier to produce than natural perfumes.

(*a*) Cinnamyl alcohol smells pleasantly of hyacinths; it can be described as unsaturated.

$$
\text{C} = \text{C} - \underset{\underset{\text{H}}{\big|}}{\overset{\overset{\text{H}}{\big|}}{\text{C}}} - \text{OH}
$$

Give **two** other terms which could be used to describe this alcohol.

Its a secondary alcohol

It contains the benzene ring.

It is aromatic

2

(*b*) Phenylethanol has a smooth rose-like odour and is used in floral perfumes together with its propanoate ester.

CH$_2$CH$_2$OH

$+$ CH$_3$CH$_2$COOH $\longrightarrow$ **X** $+$ H$_2$O

phenylethanol   propanoic acid   propanoate ester

Mass of one mole   Mass of one mole   Mass of one mole
   $= 122\,g$ $= 74\,g$ $= 178\,g$

   (i) Draw the structural formula for ester **X**.

$$
\text{H} - \underset{\underset{\text{H}}{\big|}}{\overset{\overset{\text{H}}{\big|}}{\text{C}}} - \underset{\underset{\text{H}}{\big|}}{\overset{\overset{\text{H}}{\big|}}{\text{C}}} - \overset{\overset{\text{O}}{\|}}{\text{C}} - \text{O} - \underset{\underset{\text{H}}{\big|}}{\overset{\overset{\text{H}}{\big|}}{\text{C}}} - \underset{\underset{\text{H}}{\big|}}{\overset{\overset{\text{H}}{\big|}}{\text{C}}} -
$$

1

Marks

(ii) 3·05 tonnes of phenylethanol was refluxed with 1·48 tonnes of propanoic acid.

Show, by calculation, that the phenylethanol is in excess.

(one tonne = 1000 kg)

1

(iii) The formation of the propanoate ester gives a 70% yield after refluxing.

Calculate the mass of ester obtained.

(Show your working clearly.)

2

(6)

36

Marks

13. The main source of bromine is the bromide ions in sea water. One stage in the production of bromine is shown in the diagram.

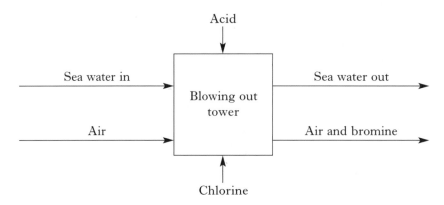

(a) Write the balanced redox equation for the displacement reaction taking place in the blowing out tower.

You may wish to refer to page 13 of the data booklet.

$$CL_2(aq) + 2e^- \rightarrow 2Cl^-(aq)$$
$$2Br^-(aq) \rightarrow Br_2(l) + 2e^-$$

1

(b) The hydrolysis of bromine to bromate ions, BrO_3^-, reduces the yield of bromine.

$$Br_2(g) \quad + \quad 6H_2O(\ell) \quad \rightleftharpoons \quad 2BrO_3^-(aq) \quad + \quad 12H^+(aq) \quad + \quad 10e$$

Why does the addition of acid to the blowing out tower slow down the hydrolysis and increase the yield of bromine?

1

(c) The majority of the world's bromine is used to make 1,2-dibromoethane, a compound added to leaded petrol.

State **one** difference between the hydrocarbons found in unleaded petrol and the hydrocarbons found in leaded petrol.

The hydrocarbons in unleaded petrol are branched.

1

(3)

Marks

14. Silver halides are used in black and white photography. Hydroquinone is a typical black and white developer which is oxidised by silver ions as follows:

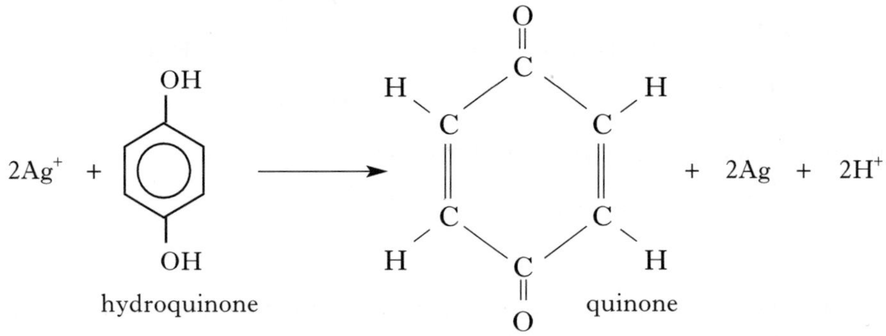

$$2Ag^+ \; + \; \text{hydroquinone} \longrightarrow \text{quinone} \; + \; 2Ag \; + \; 2H^+$$

(*a*) Write the molecular formula for hydroquinone.

$$C_6H_5(OH)_2$$

    1

(*b*) Write the ion-electron half equation for the oxidation reaction.

    1

(*c*) A saturated version of quinone, compound **X**, has the structure shown opposite.

Compound **X** can be formed by the oxidation of compound **Y**.

Draw a structural formula for compound **Y**.

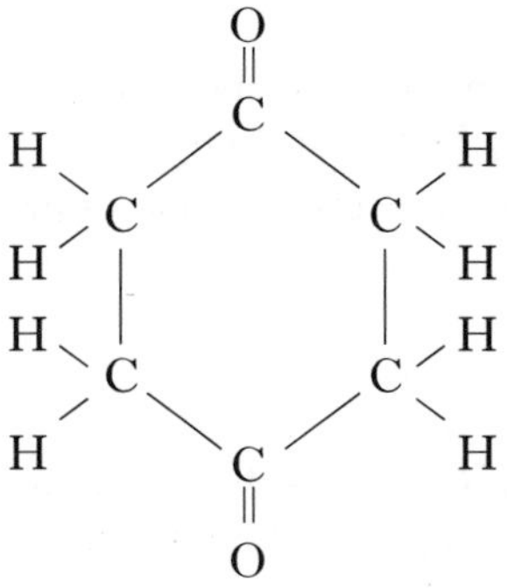

compound **X**

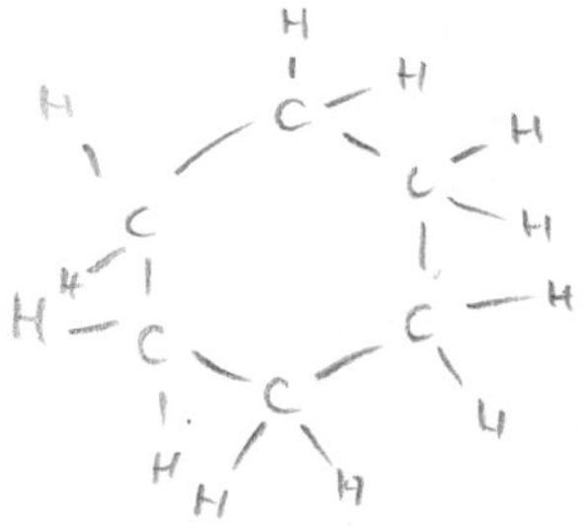

    1

    (3)

Marks

15. Ethanol can be prepared in industry by an addition reaction between steam and ethene.

$$H_2C=CH_2 \text{ (g)} + H_2O \text{ (g)} \longrightarrow CH_3CH_2OH \text{ (g)}$$

(with structural formulae drawn showing $C=C$ with H atoms and the product ethanol structure)

(*a*)   (i)   Give another name for this type of reaction.

dehydration

~~hy~~

1

(ii)   Calculate the enthalpy change for the reaction using the tables of bond enthalpies on page 11 of the data booklet.

(Show your working clearly.)

$$1 \times C=C \qquad + \quad 2 \times O-H \longrightarrow \quad 1 \times C-C \quad = \quad 337$$
$$4 \times C-H \qquad\qquad\qquad\qquad\qquad 1 \times C-O \quad = \quad 331$$
$$\qquad\qquad\qquad\qquad\qquad\qquad\qquad 1 \times O-H \quad = \quad 458$$
$$607 \qquad\qquad 2 \times 458 \qquad\qquad 5 \times C-H \quad = \quad 2070$$
$$+1656 \qquad\qquad = 916 \qquad\qquad\qquad\qquad\qquad \overline{3196}$$
$$\overline{2263} \quad + \qquad 916 \qquad\qquad \longrightarrow -3196$$

$$2263 + 916 + -3196 = \underline{-17 \text{ KJmol}^{-1}}$$

3

(*b*)   When 4 g of ethanol was dissolved in 100 cm^3 of water, the temperature rose from $17\cdot5\,°C$ to $19\cdot8\,°C$.

(i)   Give **one** method of preventing heat loss during the experiment.

Use a covered can

1

(ii)   Calculate the enthalpy of solution of ethanol using the specific heat capacity of liquid water given on page 7 of the data booklet.

(Show your working clearly.)

$$\Delta H = cm\Delta T$$
$$= 4\cdot18 \times 0\cdot1 \times 2\cdot3$$
$$\Delta H = \underline{-0\cdot9614 \text{ KJmol}^{-1}}$$

2

(7)

Marks

16. In a mass spectrometer, the energy of an electron beam can break bonds in molecules to form fragments containing groups of atoms. The positions of the peaks (or lines) in a mass spectrum correspond to the masses of the fragments which are formed.

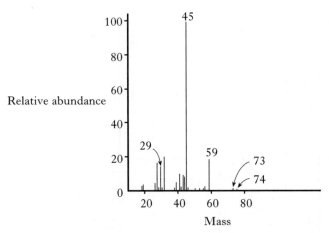

In the mass spectrum shown, the peaks at masses 29, 45 and 59 are formed by the breaking of carbon to carbon bonds in:

$$
\begin{array}{c}
\quad\ \text{H}\ \ \ \ \text{H}\ \ \ \text{H}\ \ \ \text{H} \\
\quad\ |\ \ \ \ \ |\ \ \ \ |\ \ \ \ | \\
\text{H}-\text{C}-\text{C}-\text{C}-\text{C}-\text{H} \\
\quad\ |\ \ \ \ \ |\ \ \ \ |\ \ \ \ | \\
\quad\ \text{H}\ \ \ \ \text{H}\ \ \ \text{OH}\ \text{H}
\end{array}
$$

(a) Name the above compound.

butan-2-ol

1

(b) Complete the table below.

Relative mass	Formula of fragment
29	C_2H_5
45	C_2H_4OH
59	$C_2H_{18}OH$

1

(c) What causes the peaks at masses just below the main peak at 45, eg at 44, 43, 42, 41?

1

(3)

Marks

17. Marble chips, calcium carbonate, reacted with excess dilute hydrochloric acid. The rate of reaction was followed by recording the mass of the container and the reaction mixture over a period of time.

The results of an experiment are shown in the following graph.

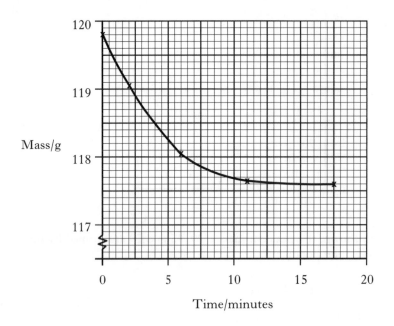

(*a*) Write a balanced equation for the reaction.

$$CaCO_3 + HCl \longrightarrow CaCl_3 + H_2$$

1

(*b*) Calculate the average rate of reaction over the first five minutes.

rate = change in mass / time

$$= \frac{119 \cdot 8 - 118 \cdot 25}{300} = \frac{1 \cdot 55}{300} = 5 \cdot 16 \times 10^{-3} \, mol\, l^{-1}s^{-1}$$

1

(*c*) Why does the average rate of reaction decrease as the reaction proceeds?

The amount of reactants get used up.

1

Marks

(d) The half-life of the reaction is the time taken for half of the calcium carbonate to be used up.

Calculate the half-life for this reaction.

$$119 \cdot 8 \div 2 = 59 \cdot 9$$

1

(e) Use the axes below to sketch a curve showing how the volume of gas produced changes over the same period of time.

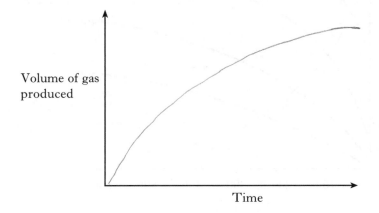

1

(5)

Marks

18. Ammonia is now one of the world's most important chemicals, about two million tonnes being produced each year in the UK alone.

It is manufactured by the direct combination of nitrogen and hydrogen by the Haber process.

$$N_2(g) \quad + \quad 3H_2(g) \quad \rightleftharpoons \quad 2NH_3(g)$$

The graph shows how the percentage of ammonia in the gas mixture at equilibrium varies with pressure at different temperatures.

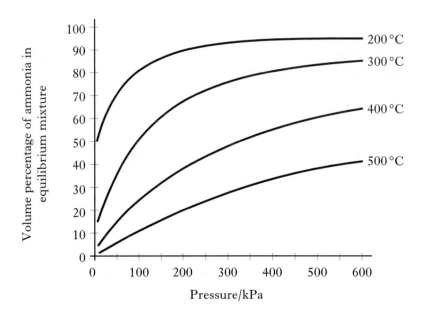

(*a*) What does the term "at equilibrium" mean?

When the rate of the forward reaction equals the rate of the backwards reaction

1

(*b*) Use the graph **and** the chemical equation to explain the conclusion that the reaction is exothermic.

More bonds have been made than have been broken.
More products than reactants

2

Marks

(*c*)   (i)   Typical conditions for the Haber process are approximately 400 °C and 200 kPa.

Use the graph to estimate the percentage of ammonia which could be obtained if the mixture was left until equilibrium was reached at this temperature and pressure.

70%

1

(ii) In practice, the percentage of ammonia in the gas mixture never rises above 15%.

Although the yield is low, the process is still profitable.

Give **one** reason for this fact.

Because the ammonia is removed to stop equilibrium being reached.

1

(5)

Marks

19. Cigarette lighter flints are composed principally of an alloy of iron and "misch" metal. One flint has a mass of $0.20\,g$. Its percentage composition by mass is shown in Table 1. Table 2 shows the percentage composition by mass of "misch" metal.

Table 1

Metal	Percentage
Misch metal	75·00
Iron	19·70
Others	5·30

Table 2

Metal	Percentage
Cerium	44·00
Lanthanum	35·00
Neodymium	12·50
Praseodymium	4·75
Others	3·75

(*a*) Calculate the mass of cerium metal in the flint.

$$0.2 \times 0.75 = 0.15g$$
$$0.15 \times 0.44 = \underline{0.066g}$$

1

(*b*) A second flint, also with a mass of $0.20\,g$, was dissolved in $30\,cm^3$ of dilute sulphuric acid, and heated with a catalyst to produce a solution containing $Ce^{4+}(aq)$ ions. The mass of cerium in this second flint was found by titrating $10\,cm^3$ of the $Ce^{4+}(aq)$ solution with iron(II) sulphate solution, using a suitable indicator.

Equations

$$Fe^{2+}(aq) \longrightarrow Fe^{3+}(aq) + e$$
$$Ce^{4+}(aq) + e \longrightarrow Ce^{3+}(aq)$$

(i) What is the purpose of the indicator?

1

Marks

(ii) 0·76 g of solid $FeSO_4$ was required to make $100\,cm^3$ of 0·05 $mol\,l^{-1}$ iron(II) sulphate solution.

Describe fully how you would prepare $100\,cm^3$ of 0·05 $mol\,l^{-1}$ iron(II) sulphate solution.

2

(iii) It was found that $4·85\,cm^3$ of 0·05 $mol\,l^{-1}$ iron(II) sulphate solution was required to reduce $10\,cm^3$ of the Ce^{4+}(aq) solution.

Calculate the mass of cerium in the flint.

(Take the relative atomic mass of cerium to be 140.)

(Show your working clearly.)

3

(7)

[END OF QUESTION PAPER]

$\dfrac{53}{90} \times 100$

$= 59\%$

SCOTTISH
CERTIFICATE OF
EDUCATION
1998

MONDAY, 18 MAY
1.00 PM – 2.40 PM

CHEMISTRY
HIGHER GRADE
Paper I

PART 1

1. Which compound contains **both** a halide ion and a transition metal ion?

   A Iron oxide

   B Silver bromide

   C Potassium permanganate

   D Copper iodate

2. In which of the following compounds do **both** ions have the same electron arrangement as argon?

   A Magnesium oxide

   B Sodium sulphide

   C Calcium bromide

   D Calcium sulphide

3. A carbohydrate did not give a colour change either when added to iodine or when warmed with Benedict's solution.

   The carbohydrate could be

   A maltose

   B sucrose

   C glucose

   D starch.

4. When copper is added to a solution containing zinc nitrate and silver nitrate

   A deposits of both zinc and silver form

   B a deposit of zinc forms

   C a deposit of silver forms

   D no new deposit forms.

5. Two experiments are set up to study the corrosion of an iron nail.

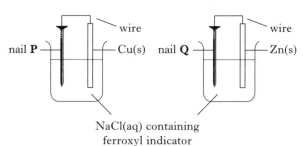

Experiment 1   Experiment 2

nail **P**   nail **Q**

wire — Cu(s)   wire — Zn(s)

NaCl(aq) containing ferroxyl indicator

   Ferroxyl indicator turns blue when $Fe^{2+}(aq)$ ions are present.

   After a short time, a blue colour will have appeared at

   A both **P** and **Q**

   B neither **P** nor **Q**

   C **P** but not at **Q**

   D **Q** but not at **P**.

6. The data shown is from the analysis of an organic compound found in meteorite rocks.

   C – 37·5 %   H – 12·5 %   O – 50%

   The empirical (simplest) formula for the compound is

   A CH_4O

   B C_3HO_4

   C $C_3H_{12}O_3$

   D CH_2O_2.

7. For any chemical, the temperature is a measure of

   A the average kinetic energy of the particles which react

   B the average kinetic energy of all the particles

   C the activation energy

   D the minimum kinetic energy required before reaction occurs.

8. An experiment was carried out at four temperatures. The table shows the times taken for the reaction to occur.

Temperature/°C	20	30	40	50
Time/s	60	30	14	5

The results show that

A the reaction is endothermic

B the activation energy increases with increasing temperature

C the rate of the reaction is directly proportional to the temperature

D a small rise in temperature results in a large increase in reaction rate.

9.

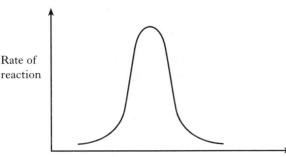

Rate of reaction

Temperature

The above diagram could represent

A the fermentation of sucrose

B neutralisation of an acid by an alkali

C the combustion of sucrose

D the reaction of a metal with acid.

10. Liquefied petroleum gas consists mainly of

A methane and ethane

B methane and butane

C propane and butane

D hexane and heptane.

11. Which mixture of gases is known as synthesis gas?

A Methane and oxygen

B Carbon monoxide and oxygen

C Carbon dioxide and hydrogen

D Carbon monoxide and hydrogen

12. Which process is used to convert methanol to methanal?

A Hydrogenation

B Condensation

C Hydration

D Oxidation

13. Oxidation of 4-methylpentan-2-ol to the corresponding ketone results in the molecule

A losing 2 g per mole

B gaining 2 g per mole

C gaining 16 g per mole

D not changing in mass.

14. Which equation could represent an industrial cracking process?

A $CH_3(CH_2)_6CH_3 \rightarrow$
$$CH_3(CH_2)_4CH_3 + CH_2 = CH_2$$

B $CH_3(CH_2)_6CH_2OH \rightarrow$
$$CH_3(CH_2)_5 CH = CH_2 + H_2O$$

C $CH_3(CH_2)_6CH_3 \rightarrow$
$$CH_3C(CH_3)_2CH_2CH(CH_3)_2$$

D $4CH_2 = CH_2 \rightarrow \quad - (CH_2CH_2)_4 -$

15. In which reaction is the volume of products less than the volume of reactants?

A $CH_4(g) + 2O_2(g) \rightarrow CO_2(g) + 2H_2O(g)$

B $2NH_3(g) \rightarrow N_2(g) + 3H_2(g)$

C $H_2(g) + Cl_2(g) \rightarrow 2HCl(g)$

D $2CO(g) + O_2(g) \rightarrow 2CO_2(g)$

16. In which of the following pairs do the gases contain the same number of atoms of oxygen?

A 1 mol of oxygen and 1 mol of carbon monoxide

B 1 mol of oxygen and 0·5 mol of carbon dioxide

C 0·5 mol of oxygen and 1 mol of carbon dioxide

D 1 mol of oxygen and 1 mol of carbon dioxide

17. A one carat diamond used in a ring contained approximately 1×10^{22} carbon atoms.

The mass of the diamond is

A 0·1 g

B 0·2 g

C 1·0 g

D 1·2 g.

18. $2NO(g) + O_2(g) \rightarrow 2NO_2(g)$

How many litres of nitrogen dioxide gas could theoretically be obtained by mixing 5 litres of nitrogen monoxide gas and 2 litres of oxygen gas?

(All volumes are measured under the same conditions of temperature and pressure.)

A 2

B 3

C 4

D 5

19. The equation shows the reaction between magnesium ribbon and dilute hydrochloric acid.

$Mg(s) + 2HCl(aq) \rightarrow MgCl_2(aq) + H_2(g)$

What volume of hydrogen will be produced when 1 g of magnesium is added to excess acid?

(Take the molar volume of hydrogen to be 24 litres mol^{-1}.)

A 1·0 litre

B 2·0 litres

C 2·4 litres

D 24·0 litres

20. Which of the following is an ester?

A

B

C

D

21. In the formation of "hardened" fats from vegetable oils, the hydrogen

A causes cross-linking between chains

B causes hydrolysis to occur

C increases the carbon chain length

D reduces the number of carbon-carbon double bonds.

22.

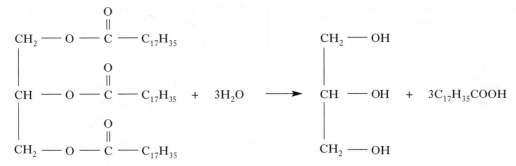

Which process is represented by the equation?

A Condensation

B Hydrolysis

C Oxidation

D Dehydration

23. What type of bond is broken when ice is melted?

A Ionic

B Polar covalent

C Hydrogen

D Non-polar covalent

24. Which element is a solid at room temperature and consists of discrete molecules?

A Carbon

B Silicon

C Sulphur

D Boron

25. Which element would require the most energy to convert one mole of gaseous atoms into gaseous ions carrying two positive charges?

(You may wish to use the data booklet.)

A Scandium

B Titanium

C Vanadium

D Chromium

26. Which compound contains hydride ions?

A HCl

B NaH

C NH_3

D H_2O

27. The shapes of some common molecules are shown below and each contains at least one polar bond.

Which of these molecules is non-polar?

A

$$Cl—\overset{\overset{\displaystyle H}{|}}{C}—Cl$$
$$\underset{Cl}{}$$

B H—Cl

C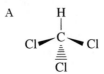

D O=C=O

28. Which oxide would be a solid at room temperature (298 K) and a gas at 600 K?

(You may wish to use the data booklet.)

A Fluorine oxide

B Phosphorus oxide

C Magnesium oxide

D Boron oxide

29. Which element has the greatest attraction for bonding electrons within a bond?

A Caesium

B Oxygen

C Fluorine

D Iodine

30. What is the relationship between a, b, c and d?

$$S(s) + H_2(g) \rightarrow H_2S(g)$$
$$\Delta H = a$$
$$H_2(g) + \tfrac{1}{2}O_2(g) \rightarrow H_2O(\ell)$$
$$\Delta H = b$$
$$S(s) + O_2(g) \rightarrow SO_2(g)$$
$$\Delta H = c$$
$$H_2S(g) + 1\tfrac{1}{2}O_2(g) \rightarrow H_2O(\ell) + SO_2(g)$$
$$\Delta H = d$$

A $a = b + c - d$

B $a = d - b - c$

C $a = b - c - d$

D $a = d + c - b$

31. A group of students added 6 g of ammonium chloride crystals to $200\,cm^3$ of water at a temperature of 25 °C.

The enthalpy of solution of ammonium chloride is $+13 \cdot 6\,kJ\,mol^{-1}$.

After dissolving the crystals, the temperature of the solution would most likely be

A 23 °C

B 25 °C

C 27 °C

D 30 °C.

32. Which equation illustrates an enthalpy of combustion?

A $C_2H_6(g) + 3\tfrac{1}{2}O_2(g)$
$\rightarrow 2CO_2(g) + 3H_2O(\ell)$

B $C_2H_5OH(\ell) + O_2(g)$
$\rightarrow CH_3COOH(\ell) + H_2O(\ell)$

C $CH_3CHO(\ell) + \tfrac{1}{2}O_2(g)$
$\rightarrow CH_3COOH(\ell)$

D $CH_4(g) + 1\tfrac{1}{2}O_2(g)$
$\rightarrow CO(g) + 2H_2O(\ell)$

33. In the presence of bright light, hydrogen and chlorine react explosively. One step in the reaction is shown below.

$$H_2(g) + Cl(g) \rightarrow HCl(g) + H(g)$$

Using page 11 of the data booklet, the enthalpy change, in $kJ\,mol^{-1}$, for this step is calculated as

A 5

B 193

C 679

D 867.

34. When a reversible chemical reaction is at equilibrium,

A the concentrations of reactants and products remain equal

B the forward reaction is unable to continue

C the concentrations of reactants and products remain constant

D the forward and reverse reactions proceed at different rates.

35. A catalyst is added to a reaction at equilibrium.

Which of the following does **not** apply?

A The rate of the forward reaction increases.

B The rate of the reverse reaction increases.

C The position of equilibrium remains unchanged.

D The position of equilibrium shifts to the right.

36. A liquid has a pH value of 10.

What is the concentration of $H^+(aq)$ ions present, in $mol\,l^{-1}$?

A 10^{-10}

B 1

C 100

D 10^{10}

37. Excess marble chips (calcium carbonate) were added to $100\,cm^3$ of $1\,mol\,l^{-1}$ hydrochloric acid. The experiment was repeated using the same mass of the marble chips and $100\,cm^3$ of $1\,mol\,l^{-1}$ ethanoic acid.

Which would have been the same for both experiments?

A The time taken for the reaction to be completed

B The rate at which the first $10\,cm^3$ of gas is evolved

C The mass of marble chips left over when reaction has stopped

D The average rate of the reaction

38. The half-life of 1 g bismuth oxide compared to 1 g bismuth sulphate will be

A greater because the percentage of bismuth is greater

B less because of the greater stability of the smaller oxide ion

C the same because the half-life is independent of the percentage of bismuth

D impossible to predict.

39. What is the result of an atom losing a β-particle?

	Atomic number	Mass number
A	increased	no change
B	decreased	no change
C	no change	increased
D	no change	decreased

40. Induced nuclear reactions can be described in a shortened form

$$T\,(x, y)\,P$$

where the participants are the target nucleus (T), the bombarding particle (x), the ejected particle (y) and the product nucleus (P).

Which nuclear reaction would **not** give the product nucleus indicated?

A $^{14}_{7}N$ (α, p) $^{17}_{8}O$

B $^{242}_{96}Cf$ (n, α) $^{239}_{94}Pu$

C $^{10}_{5}B$ (α, n) $^{13}_{7}N$

D $^{236}_{93}Np$ (p, α) $^{238}_{92}U$

PART 2

In questions 41 to 47 of this part of the paper, an answer is given by circling the appropriate letter (or letters) in the answer grids provided on Part 2 of the answer sheet.

In some questions, two letters are required for full marks.

If more than the correct number of answers is given, marks may be deducted.

In some cases the number of correct responses is NOT identified in the question.

This part of the paper is worth 20 marks.

41. Many organic functional groups contain oxygen.

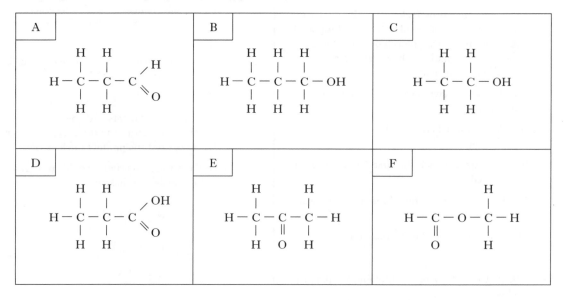

(*a*) Identify the aldehyde.

(*b*) Identify the compound which could be hydrolysed when warmed with sodium hydroxide solution.

(*c*) Identify the **two** compounds which could be oxidised to produce the compound shown in box **D**.

(*d*) Identify the **two** isomers.

42. Nuclear transformations involve different processes.

A		B		C	
alpha emission		beta emission		neutron capture	
D		E		F	
proton capture		nuclear fusion		nuclear fission	

Identify the process taking place in each of the transformations.

(*a*) $^{23}_{11}\text{Na} + x \rightarrow ^{24}_{11}\text{Na}$

(*b*) $^{2}_{1}\text{H} + ^{3}_{1}\text{H} \rightarrow ^{4}_{2}\text{He} + y$

43.

$$CH_3 - CH_2 - C\!\!\!\diagup_{\!\!\!H}^{\!\!\!O} \quad \xrightarrow{\quad X \quad} \quad CH_3 - CH_2 - CH_2 - OH \quad \xrightarrow{\quad Y \quad} \quad CH_3 - CH = CH_2$$

A		B		C	
	Oxidation		Reduction		Hydrogenation
D		E		F	
	Dehydrogenation		Dehydration		Condensation

(a) Identify the name which could be applied to reaction **Y**.

(b) Identify the name(s) which could be applied to reaction **X**.

44. The properties of oxides are related to their bonding and structures.

A		B		C	
	Na_2O		P_4O_{10}		H_2O
D		E		F	
	Al_2O_3		Fe_2O_3		CuO

(a) Identify the **two** oxides which are made up of discrete molecules.

(b) Identify the oxide which would dissolve in water to produce a solution with pH greater than 7.

(c) Identify the oxide(s) which would react with sodium hydroxide solution.

45. Changes in concentration can alter the position of an equilibrium.

$$Cl_2\,(aq) \quad + \quad H_2O\,(\ell) \quad \rightleftharpoons \quad 2H^+(aq) \quad + \quad ClO^-(aq) \quad + \quad Cl^-(aq)$$

A		B		C	
	$KCl(s)$		$KOH(s)$		$Na_2SO_4(s)$
D		E		F	
	$AgNO_3(s)$		$KF(s)$		$NaNO_3(s)$

(a) Identify the compound which if added to the equilibrium mixture would move the equilibrium to the left.

(b) Identify the compound(s) which if added to the equilibrium mixture would move the equilibrium to the right.

46. Lithium hydride is produced by the reaction of lithium with hydrogen.

$$Li(s) \quad + \quad \tfrac{1}{2}H_2(g) \quad \rightarrow \quad LiH(s) \qquad \Delta H \; = \; -90 kJ\, mol^{-1}$$

Identify the true statement(s).

A	The reaction is endothermic.
B	The reaction to produce lithium hydride is a redox action.
C	The energy change in the reaction represents the enthalpy of formation of lithium hydride.
D	Lithium hydride has metallic bonding.
E	Lithium hydride has hydrogen bonding.
F	The electrolysis of lithium hydride melt produces hydrogen at the negative electrode.

47. The value for the Avogadro constant is $6 \cdot 02 \times 10^{23}\, mol^{-1}$.

Identify the true statement(s).

A	There are $6 \cdot 02 \times 10^{23}$ atoms in $0 \cdot 5\, mol$ of neon gas.
B	There are $6 \cdot 02 \times 10^{23}$ electrons in $0 \cdot 5\, mol$ of hydrogen gas.
C	There are $6 \cdot 02 \times 10^{23}$ molecules in $0 \cdot 5\, mol$ of oxygen gas.
D	There are $6 \cdot 02 \times 10^{23}$ hydrogen atoms in $0 \cdot 5\, mol$ of water.
E	There are $6 \cdot 02 \times 10^{23}$ oxide ions in $0 \cdot 5\, mol$ of potassium oxide.
F	There are $6 \cdot 02 \times 10^{23}$ sodium ions in $0 \cdot 5\, mol$ of sodium chloride.

[END OF QUESTION PAPER]

SCOTTISH
CERTIFICATE OF
EDUCATION
1998

MONDAY, 18 MAY
9.30 AM – 12.00 NOON

CHEMISTRY
HIGHER GRADE
Paper II

1. (*a*) Hydrocarbons which are suitable for unleaded petrol are produced in oil *Marks*
refineries. An example of one of the reactions which takes place is shown.

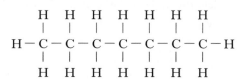

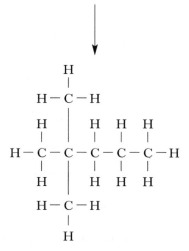

(i) What name is given to the industrial process in which reactions like the
above occur?

reforming

1

(ii) State the systematic name for the product of the reaction shown.

2,2 - dimethylpentane

1

(iii) What structural feature of the product makes it suitable for use in
unleaded petrol?

The branches

1

(*b*) Oil refineries also produce diesel fuel.

How does the method of ignition of diesel in a car engine differ from that of
ignition of petrol?

*Diesel can be compressed and ignites
spontaneously, while petrol is
ignited with a spark.*

1

(4)

Marks

2. In spacecraft, the total mass carried and the air quality are important. Lithium hydroxide has been used to absorb carbon dioxide produced by astronauts. The equation for the reaction is:

$$LiOH \quad + \quad CO_2 \quad \longrightarrow \quad LiHCO_3$$

(*a*) 6·0 g of lithium hydroxide absorbs 5·9 litres of carbon dioxide.

Use this information to calculate the molar volume of carbon dioxide.

(Show your working clearly.)

$$molar\ volume = \frac{molar\ mass}{density}$$

2

(*b*) Lithium hydroxide is more expensive and less common than sodium hydroxide.

Suggest why lithium hydroxide is still preferred to sodium hydroxide for use in spacecraft.

Lithium is lighter than sodium.

1

(3)

Marks

3. Proteins are polymers found in the human body in tissues such as hair, finger nails and skin.

(a) Name the type of compound produced by hydrolysis of a protein.

amino acid

1

(b) Part of a protein molecule is shown.

$$
\begin{array}{ccccccccc}
\text{H} & \text{H} & \text{O} & \text{H} & \text{H} & \text{O} & \text{H} & \text{H} & \text{O} & \text{H} \\
| & | & \| & | & | & \| & | & | & \| & | \\
-\text{N} & -\text{C} & -\text{C} & -\text{N} & -\text{C} & -\text{C} & -\text{N} & -\text{C} & -\text{C} & -\text{N}- \\
& | & & & | & & & | & & \\
& \text{H} & & & \text{CH}_2 & & & \text{CH}_2 & & \\
& & & & | & & & | & & \\
& & & & \text{COOH} & & & \text{S} & & \\
& & & & & & & | & & \\
& & & & & & & \text{H} & &
\end{array}
$$

Draw the structural formula for **one** of the monomers produced by hydrolysis of this protein fragment.

H — N — C — C — OH (amino acid structure with H, H, O above)

1

(c) Proteins can be denatured by heat.
What is meant by denatured?

Heat changes the shape of the enzymes, so they can no longer work for their reactions.

1

(3)

Marks

4. The syringe shown was used to study the reactions of hydrocarbons with oxygen at a constant temperature of 120 °C.

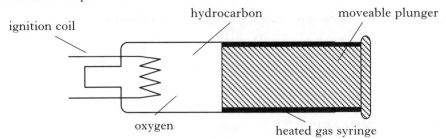

hydrocarbon   moveable plunger

ignition coil

oxygen

heated gas syringe

In one experiment, $20 \, cm^3$ of a hydrocarbon gas containing six carbon atoms per molecule was ignited in excess oxygen gas. Carbon dioxide and water vapour were produced.

(a) Calculate the volume of carbon dioxide gas produced.

$$C_6H_{14} + O_2 \rightarrow 6CO_2 + 7H_2O$$

1

(b) $100 \, cm^3$ of water vapour was produced.

What is the molecular formula for the hydrocarbon?

1

(2)

Marks

5. Hydrogen peroxide can be used to clean contact lenses. In this process, the enzyme catalase is added to break down hydrogen peroxide.

The equation for the reaction is:

$$2H_2O_2 \longrightarrow 2H_2O + O_2$$

The rate of oxygen production was measured in three laboratory experiments using the same volume of hydrogen peroxide at the same temperature.

Experiment	Concentration of H_2O_2/mol l^{-1}	Catalyst used
A	0·2	yes
B	0·4	yes
C	0·2	no

The curve obtained for experiment **A** is shown.

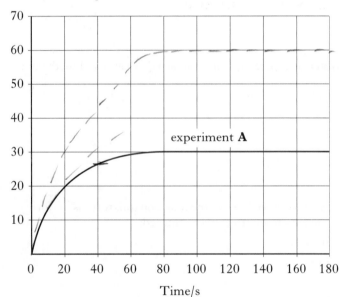

(*a*) Calculate the average rate of the reaction over the first 40 s.

$$\frac{27}{40} = 0.675 \text{ mol l}^{-1} \text{ s}^{-1}$$

1

(*b*) Add curves to the graph to show the results of experiments **B** and **C**.
Label each curve clearly.

2

(*c*) Draw a labelled diagram of assembled laboratory apparatus which could be used to carry out these experiments.

1

(4)

Marks

6. Esters are important and useful compounds. They occur in nature and can also be made in the laboratory.

(*a*) An ester can be made from ethanol and methanoic acid.
Draw the full structural formula for this ester.

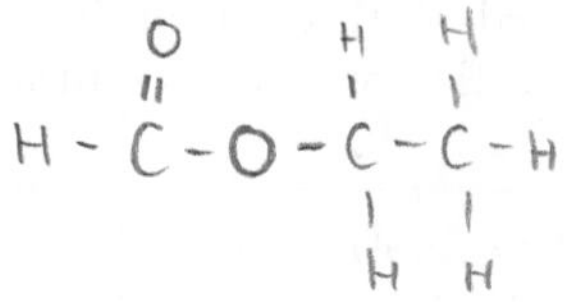

$$H - \overset{\overset{\textstyle O}{\|}}{C} - O - \overset{\overset{\textstyle H}{|}}{\underset{\underset{\textstyle H}{|}}{C}} - \overset{\overset{\textstyle H}{|}}{\underset{\underset{\textstyle H}{|}}{C}} - H$$

1

(*b*) Name the catalyst used in the laboratory preparation of an ester.

Sulphuric acid

1

(*c*) How can this ester be separated from unreacted ethanol and methanoic acid?

1

(*d*) Unless the ester is removed from the reaction mixture as it forms, 100% conversion of reactants to ester is never achieved.
Give a reason for this.

1

(4)

7. Radioisotopes are used in the treatment of patients suffering from cancer.

(*a*) The isotope $^{60}_{27}\text{Co}$ has a half-life of 5·3 years and is used to supply gamma radiation from outside the body of the patient.

Give **two** reasons why this isotope would **not** be suitable for use inside the body.

Its half-life is too long.

2

(*b*) $^{32}_{15}\text{P}$, a beta-emitting isotope with a half-life of 14 days, is used in the treatment of skin cancer.

(i) Show, **by calculation**, how the proton to neutron ratio is changed by the decay of this isotope.

$$^{32}_{15}\text{P} \longrightarrow \, ^{32}_{16}\text{S} + \, ^{0}_{-1}\text{e}$$

The decay of the isotope causes the ratio to fall to 1 proton : 1 neutron.

1

(ii) 3 g of the isotope was used to treat cancer over a period of 56 days. Calculate the mass of the isotope which decayed during this time.

3g = 100%   56÷14 = 4 half lifes

1·5g = 50%

0·75g = 25%

0·375g = 12·5%

0·1875g = 6·25%

1
(4)

0·1875g left so 3 − 0·1875 = 2·8125 g decayed

Marks

8. A pupil found the enthalpy of combustion of propan-1-ol using the following apparatus.

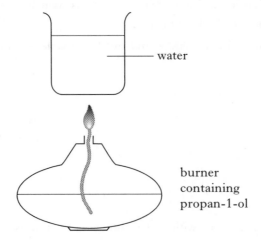

water

burner
containing
propan-1-ol

(*a*) In addition to the initial and final temperatures of the water, what other measurements would the pupil have made?

weight of burner before and
weight of burner after

2

(*b*) The table shows enthalpies of combustion of three alcohols.

Compound	Enthalpy of combustion/$kJ\,mol^{-1}$
methanol	−715
ethanol	−1371
propan-1-ol	−2010

Why is there a **regular** increase in enthalpies of combustion from methanol to ethanol to propan-1-ol?

1

(*c*) The equation for the enthalpy of formation of propan-1-ol is:

$$3C(s) \quad + \quad 4H_2(g) \quad + \quad \tfrac{1}{2}O_2(g) \quad \longrightarrow \quad C_3H_7OH\,(\ell)$$

Use information on enthalpies of combustion from the data booklet to calculate the enthalpy of formation of propan-1-ol.

(Show your working clearly.)

3

(6)

Marks

9. Ethane-1,2-diol is a colourless liquid used as anti-freeze in car radiators. It can be made in the laboratory from ethene.

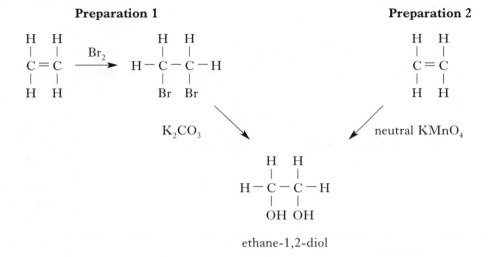

ethane-1,2-diol

(a) Give the traditional name for ethane-1,2-diol.

ethylene glycol

1

(b) In preparation 1, the reaction of K_2CO_3 produces the salt potassium bromide and carbon dioxide as by-products.

Give the formula for another compound, **not containing carbon**, which would react with K_2CO_3 to produce the same salt and carbon dioxide.

$$K_2CO_3 + BrOH \rightarrow KBr + CO_2 + C_2H_4(OH)_2$$

1

(c) In preparation 2, the $KMnO_4$ oxidises ethene in **neutral** aqueous solution. Complete the balancing of the ion-electron equation shown.

$$MnO_4^-(aq) + 2H_2O + 3e^- \longrightarrow MnO_2(s) + 4OH^-(aq)$$

1

(d) Ethane-1,2-diol can be polymerised with terephthalic acid to form a condensation polymer.

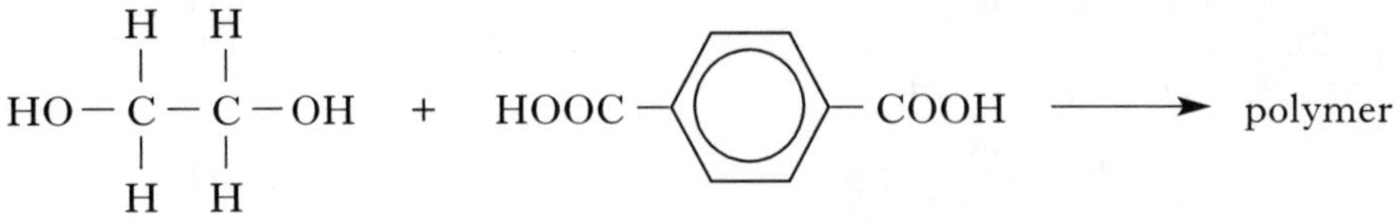

$$\text{HO}-\underset{\underset{\text{H}}{|}}{\overset{\overset{\text{H}}{|}}{\text{C}}}-\underset{\underset{\text{H}}{|}}{\overset{\overset{\text{H}}{|}}{\text{C}}}-\text{OH} \quad + \quad \text{HOOC}-\bigcirc-\text{COOH} \quad \longrightarrow \quad \text{polymer}$$

terephthalic acid

(i) Write the molecular formula for terephthalic acid.

$$C_6H_6(COOH)_2$$

1

(ii) Draw a section of polymer showing **one** molecule of each monomer joined together.

1

(iii) Why would this polymer be formed as a fibre and **not** a resin?

1

(6)

Marks

10. The structural formulae for some acids containing oxygen are shown.

Acid	Strength	Structure
carbonic	weak	$HO-C{\overset{\displaystyle O}{\underset{OH}{\diagup\!\!\!\!/}}}$
ethanoic	weak	$CH_3-C{\overset{\displaystyle O}{\underset{OH}{\diagup\!\!\!\!/}}}$
nitric	strong	$O{\overset{O}{\underset{\diagdown}{\diagup}}}N-OH$
nitrous	weak	$O=N-OH$
sulphuric	strong	$\underset{O{\diagup}\,\diagdown OH}{\overset{O{\diagdown}\,\diagup OH}{S}}$
sulphurous	weak	$HO-S{\overset{\displaystyle O}{\underset{OH}{\diagup\!\!\!\!/}}}$

(a) (i) Describe **two** tests to distinguish between a weak acid and a strong acid, stating clearly the result of each test.

Test 1   take their pH

a weak acid – has a pH just below 7

a strong acid – has a pH well below 7

Test 2   test their reaction with magnesium

they will both react to release H_2

a weak acid – less vigorous

a strong acid – more vigorous

2

Marks

(ii) State the **two** variables which must be controlled in **both** tests to make the tests fair.

concentration of both acids
volume of both acids

1

(b) What structural feature appears to determine the strength of these acids?

Strong acids have two carbonyl groups
weak acids only have one

1

(c) Chloric acid, $HClO_3$, is a strong acid.
Draw its full structural formula.

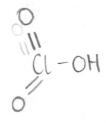

1

(d) Estimate the pH of 0·008 mol l^{-1} nitric acid solution.

$0.008 = 8 \times 10^{-3}$

1

(e) Carbonic acid forms a salt, sodium carbonate.
Explain why sodium carbonate solution is alkaline.

2

(8)

Marks

11. Ammonia is made by the Haber Process.

$$N_2(g) \quad + \quad 3H_2(g) \quad \rightleftharpoons \quad 2NH_3(g)$$

(*a*) The Haber Process is normally carried out at 200 atmospheres pressure.

Suggest **one** advantage and **one** disadvantage of increasing the pressure in the Haber Process beyond 200 atmospheres.

Increasing the pressure speeds up the getting to equilibrium.
Increasing the pressure lowers the yield of ammonia. **1**

(*b*) The activation energy (E_A) and enthalpy change (ΔH) for this reaction are $236 \, kJ \, mol^{-1}$ and $-92 \, kJ \, mol^{-1}$ respectively.

(i) Use this information to draw the potential energy diagram for the reaction.

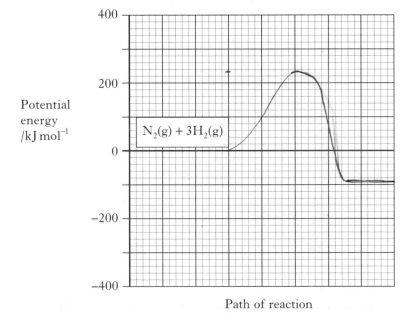

Path of reaction **1**

(ii) Calculate the activation energy for the reverse reaction.

$92 + 236 = 328 \, KJmol^{-1}$

1

(*c*) Over a period of time, 120 tonnes of hydrogen produced 88·4 tonnes of ammonia by the Haber Process.

Calculate the percentage yield of ammonia.

(1 tonne = 1000 kg)

(Show your working clearly.)

2

(5)

Marks

12. Methanol and ethanol can be used as alternative fuels in car engines.

(*a*) **Methanol**

Methanol can be made as follows.

$$X \quad + \quad H_2O \quad \xrightarrow{\text{steam reforming}} \quad CO \quad + \quad 3H_2 \quad \longrightarrow \quad CH_3OH$$

synthesis gas

(i) Identify **X**.

Carbon

1

(ii) Methanol is less volatile than petrol and less likely to explode in a car accident.

Explain why methanol is less volatile than petrol.

2

(*b*) **Ethanol**

In some countries, ethanol for fuel is made by fermentation.

(i) Why is ethanol considered to be a "renewable" fuel?

Ethanol can be formed by the fermentation of sugar.

Sugar can be grown afresh each year. i.e. renewable

1

(ii) To meet market demand, ethanol is also made by a method other than fermentation.

What is this method?

the hydration of ethene.

1

(5)

Marks

13. Titanium is a very useful metal. It has many uses, from components of spacecraft to spectacle frames.

The diagram shows steps in the manufacture of titanium.

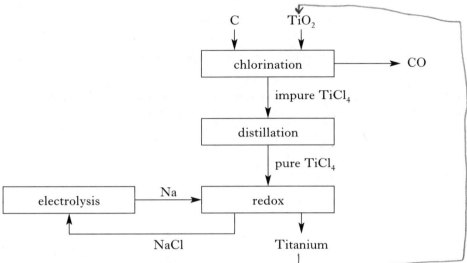

(a) In this diagram, sodium is recycled.

Add a labelled arrow to the diagram to show how another chemical is recycled.

1

(b) $TiCl_4$ can be separated from impurities by fractional distillation because it is volatile.

What does this suggest about the type of bonding in $TiCl_4$?

1

(c) During the distillation step, care must be taken to ensure that no water enters the reaction chamber.

What type of reaction is this designed to prevent?

1

(d) Give another name for the redox reaction to produce titanium.

1

(4)

Marks

14. For people who suffer from bronchitis, even low concentrations of ozone, O_3, irritate the lining of the throat and can cause headaches.

NO$_2$ gas from car exhausts reacts with oxygen to form ozone as follows.

$$O_2(g) \quad + \quad NO_2(g) \quad \rightleftharpoons \quad NO(g) \quad + \quad O_3(g)$$

Car exhaust fumes also contain volatile organic compounds (VOCs), which can combine with NO gas.

(*a*) Explain how a rise in VOC concentration will change the ozone concentration.

1

(*b*) In an experiment to measure the ozone concentration of air in a Scottish city, 10^5 litres of air were bubbled through a solution of potassium iodide. Ozone reacts with potassium iodide solution, releasing iodine.

$$2KI(aq) \quad + \quad O_3(g) \quad + \quad H_2O(\ell) \quad \longrightarrow \quad I_2(aq) \quad + \quad O_2(g) \quad + \quad 2KOH(aq)$$

The iodine formed was titrated with $0{\cdot}01$ mol l^{-1} sodium thiosulphate solution, Na$_2$S$_2$O$_3$(aq), using starch indicator.

$$I_2(aq) \quad + \quad 2S_2O_3^{2-}(aq) \quad \longrightarrow \quad 2I^-(aq) \quad + \quad S_4O_6^{2-}(aq)$$

The results of three titrations are shown in the table.

Experiment	Volume of thiosulphate/cm^3
1	22·90
2	22·40
3	22·50

(i) What colour change would show that the titration was complete?

yellow → brown

1

Marks

(ii) Why was the volume of sodium thiosulphate to be used in the calculation taken to be $22 \cdot 45 \, \text{cm}^3$ although this is **not** the average of the three titres in the table?

1

(iii) Taking the volume of sodium thiosulphate solution to be $22 \cdot 45 \, \text{cm}^3$, calculate the volume of ozone in **one litre** of air.

(Take the molar volume of ozone to be 24 litres mol^{-1}.)

(Show your working clearly.)

3

(6)

Marks

15. The Scottish chemist, Sir William Ramsay, discovered the element argon in air in 1894 by removing all oxygen, carbon dioxide and water vapour from air. He thought that the remaining gas would be pure nitrogen but it was denser than the nitrogen made by the thermal decomposition of ammonium nitrite, NH_4NO_2.

The equation for this decomposition reaction is

$$NH_4NO_2 \longrightarrow N_2 + 2H_2O$$

(a) (i) Suggest why argon was not discovered until 1894.

1

   (ii) Why was the nitrogen from air denser than that from the decomposition of ammonium nitrite?

1

(b) One way of removing water vapour from air involves passing moist air over magnesium nitride. Water reacts with magnesium nitride to form ammonia and magnesium oxide.

Write a balanced equation for this reaction.

1

(c) A sample of air contains 23·2% by mass of oxygen.

Calculate the number of oxygen atoms present in 100 g of air.

(Show your working clearly.)

$1 \text{ mol} \rightarrow 16g \rightarrow 6.02 \times 10^{23}$

$100 \times 0.232 = 23.2g$

$16g \rightarrow 6.02 \times 10^{23}$

$1 \rightarrow \dfrac{6.02 \times 10^{23}}{16}$

$23.2 \rightarrow \dfrac{6.02 \times 10^{23}}{16} \times 23.2g$

$\Rightarrow 8.729 \times 10^{23} \text{ atoms}$

2

(5)

Marks

16. Gases are produced by the electrolysis of $Na_2SO_4(aq)$.

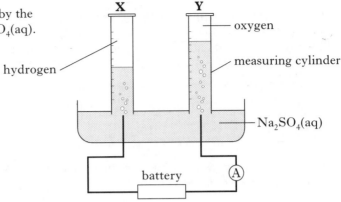

The ion-electron equations are shown.

Electrode **X**: $2H_2O(\ell) + 2e^- \longrightarrow H_2(g) + 2OH^-(aq)$

Electrode **Y**: $H_2O(\ell) \longrightarrow \frac{1}{2}O_2(g) + 2H^+(aq) + 2e^-$

(*a*) Explain what happens to the pH at each electrode.

Electrode **X**:   The pH ~~decreases~~ increases

Electrode **Y**:   The pH decreases

1

(*b*) A current of 2A was passed through the apparatus for 5 min and 20 s.
Calculate the volume of hydrogen gas produced.
(Take the molar volume of hydrogen gas to be 24 litres mol^{-1}.)
(Show your working clearly.)

$Q = I \times t$
$Q = 2 \times 320$
$Q = 640\ C$

3

(4)

Marks

17. Bond enthalpies and boiling points of some halogens are shown in the table.

Halogen	Bond enthalpy/kJ mol^{-1}	Boiling point/K
Cl — Cl	243	238
Br — Br	194	332
I — I	161	457

(a) Why do the boiling points of the halogens increase down the group, although the covalent bonds become weaker?

Because Van der Waals increases

1

(b) Enthalpy of formation values and bond enthalpies for some hydrogen halides are shown in the table.

Halide	Enthalpy of formation /kJ mol^{-1}	Bond enthalpy/kJ mol^{-1}
H — F	−271	569
H — Cl	−92	431
H — Br	−36	366
H — I	+26	299

(i) What do the enthalpy of formation values indicate about the stability of hydrogen halides?

1

(ii) Explain why the value for the enthalpy of formation for HCl is so different from its bond enthalpy.

Your answer must include relevant equations.

2

(4)

Marks

18. Acrolein is a feedstock for the production of useful organic compounds, eg acrylic fibres, synthetic rubber and glycerol.

Acrolein was first produced after the Second World War by oxidation of propene using an antimony catalyst as shown in the first stage of the diagram.

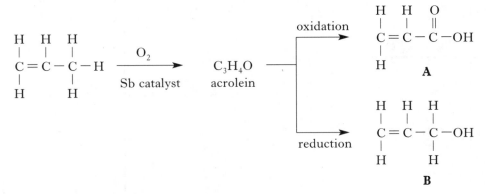

(*a*) Draw the full structural formula for acrolein.

1

(*b*) **Four** experiments were carried out on compounds **A** and **B**.

Complete the table to predict the results of these experiments.

Experiment	Compound **A**	Compound **B**
Reaction with sodium	Hydrogen gas given off	Hydrogen gas given off
Solubility in water	Soluble	Soluble
pH	Less than seven	Neutral
Reaction with magnesium	Hydrogen gas given off	

2

(*c*) Compound **B** has an isomer which belongs to a different homologous series and has **no effect** on Benedict's (or Fehling's) solution.

Draw the full structural formula for this isomer.

1

(4)

Marks

19. The diagram, **which is not drawn to scale**, can be used to calculate the enthalpy of formation of lithium fluoride. All energy changes are in kJ.

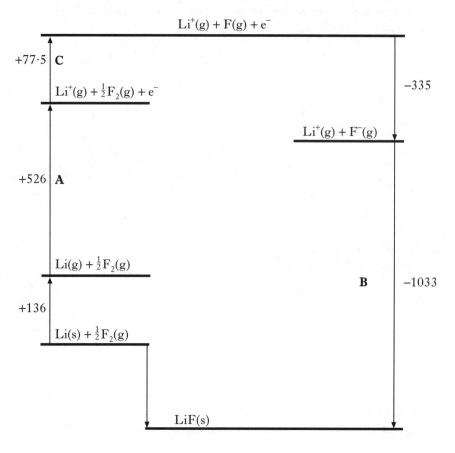

(a) Name the energy changes **A** and **B**.

   A   1st ionisation energy

   B   Lattice formation

2

(b) Calculate the enthalpy of formation of lithium fluoride.

   $-1033 + -335 =$

1